BBC ACTIVE

KS3 BITESIZE revision

Key

English

Complete Revision Guide

Steve Eddy

Published by BBC Active, an imprint of Educational Publishers LLP, part of the Pearson Education Group
Edinburgh Gate, Harlow, Essex CN20 2JE, England

ISBN: 978-1-4066-1382-7

Illustrations by Richard Smith

Printed in China GCC/01

The Publisher's policy is to use paper ... ests.

First published 2003
This edition 2007

CHECK ON
ISSUE & RETURN

KU-490-334

Contents

Acknowledgements

Every effort has been made to contact copyright holders. The publishers would like to thank the following for permission to reproduce text:

Pages 6 and 13: *Black Elk Speaks* Reprinted from *Black Elk Speaks: Being the Life Story of a Holy Man of the Oglala Sioux* as told through John G. Neihardt (Flaming Rainbow) by Nicholas Black Elk by permission of the University of Nebraska Press. Copyright © 1961 by the John G. Neihardt Trust. © 2000 by the University of Nebraska.

Page 6: *The Diary of a Young Girl: The Definitive Edition* by Anne Frank, edited by Otto H Frank and Mirjam Pressler,

translated by Susan Massotty (Viking, 1997) copyright © The Anne Frank-Fonds, Basle, Switzerland, 1991. English translation copyright © Doubleday, a division of Bantam Doubleday Dell Publishing Group Inc, 1995.

Page 6: *Karl Marx*, Francis Wheen, HarperCollins Publishers Ltd © 2000, Francis Wheen.

Page 7: *A Walk in the Woods* © Bill Bryson. Extract from *A Walk in the Woods* by Bill Bryson, published by Black Swan, a division of Transworld Publishers. All rights reserved.

Page 11: *The Baby and Fly Pie* © Melvin Burgess, *The Baby and Fly Pie*, Andersen Press Ltd.

Page 13: Extract from *Brother in the Land* by Robert Swindells, copyright © Robert Swindells 1984, reprinted by permission of Oxford University Press.

Page 17: *Holes*, Louis Sachar, Bloomsbury.

Page 21: *Stone Cold* by Robert Swindells (Hamish Hamilton, 1993). Copyright © Robert Swindells, 1993.

Page 22: Reprinted by arrangement with the Estate of Martin Luther King Jr., c/o Writers House as agent for the proprietor New York, NY. *Copyright 1963 Dr. Martin Luther King Jr., copyright renewed 1991 Coretta Scott King*

Page 25: *'Tis*, Frank McCourt. HarperCollins Publishers Ltd © 2000, Frank McCourt.

About *Bitesize*

The BBC revision service, *KS3 Bitesize*, is designed to help you achieve success in the KS3 National Tests.

It includes books, television programmes and a website at **www.bbc.co.uk/education/ks3bitesize**.

Each of these works as a separate resource, designed to help you get the best results.

The television programmes are available on video through your school or you can find out transmission times by calling **08700 100 222**.

About this book

This book is your all-in-one revision companion for the KS3 National Tests. It gives you the three things you need for successful revision:

1 every topic clearly organised and clearly explained

2 the most important facts and ideas highlighted for quick checking

3 all the practice you need.

This book contains a complete set of revision information for pupils taking the KS3 English tests.

The main areas of English are broken down into several topics. Each topic has a double page in the book. The format of each topic is the same, so you can find your way around easily. The features you can find in each topic are described here:

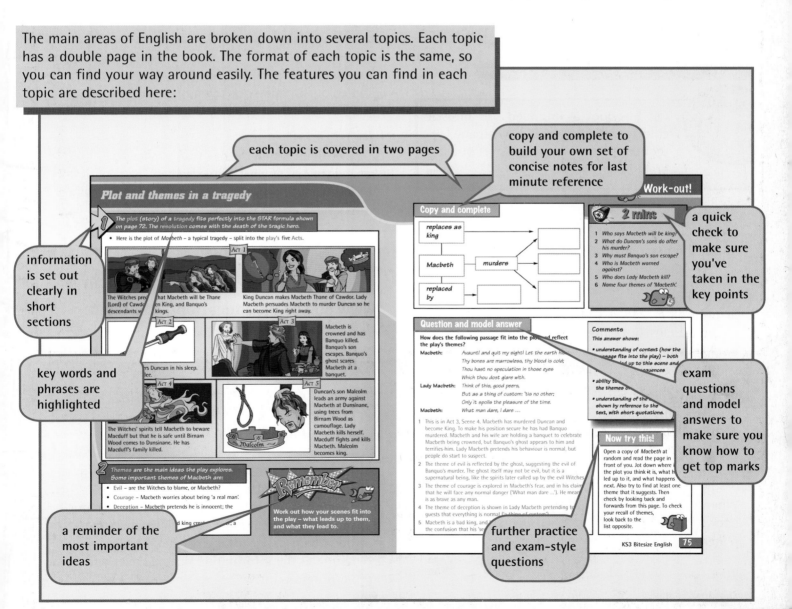

each topic is covered in two pages

copy and complete to build your own set of concise notes for last minute reference

information is set out clearly in short sections

key words and phrases are highlighted

a reminder of the most important ideas

a quick check to make sure you've taken in the key points

exam questions and model answers to make sure you know how to get top marks

further practice and exam-style questions

In English you will have **three** separate tests. These are:

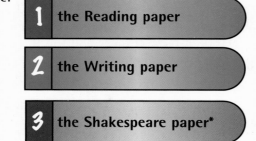

1 the Reading paper

2 the Writing paper

3 the Shakespeare paper*

These tests will be grouped together over two or three days. Each one tests a different aspect of your ability to use and appreciate written English. You will be given separate assessments for Reading and Writing. The examiner marking the Reading paper will be looking for evidence of how well you have understood what you have read – not how well you can write. The test of how well you express yourself in writing comes in the Writing paper. The Shakespeare paper tests your knowledge and understanding of one Shakespeare play, focusing on two sections of that play.

(*In Wales, formal tests have been replaced by teacher assessment.)

Revising for English

tips

Use this book as intended – in 'bitesize' chunks. Work through a two-page section, then have a rest to let your brain take it all in.

Try working with a friend and testing each other, or getting a parent to test you.

Skim through the left-hand page before and after reading it closely, paying special attention to the **bold** keywords.

Do try to find time for the 'Now try this!' sections. Your brain learns best by taking an active approach – not just reading.

When you've worked through a section once, go back to it the next day and see how much you remember. You could try the '2 mins' test again.

You could make the 'Copy and complete' cards big and colourful and stick them on your wall.

In quiet times during the day, take a moment to remind yourself of what you've learned. Once you've reminded yourself several times, information will stay in your memory and come back to you like magic in the test!

Use the *Bitesize* website to back up your learning:

www.bbc.co.uk/education/ks3bitesize

Waiting for the test to start

If you're nervous, take a few deep, slow, deliberate breaths to calm yourself down. Remind yourself that you probably know much more than you realise. You're not allowed to open your paper until you're told to, but you can read the information on the cover and fill in your details.

What to take with you

You need:

- at least one reliable pen – preferably two, just in case

- pencil, sharpener and eraser (if you think you might work in pencil)

- ruler (optional)

- highlighter pen (optional but useful for marking phrases in the text for your own attention).

You don't need:

- a dictionary, thesaurus or spellchecker – they're not allowed

- the Shakespeare play you're studying – the passages are provided

- paper – you write in a booklet, and the teacher in charge will have spare paper if you need it.

The tests in detail

Reading test

This test lasts **1 hour** and **15 minutes**, including 15 minutes reading time. It carries 32 marks. You'll be given a booklet of three texts. These will be connected in some way, but contrasting in style and approach. For example, there might be part of a story about bungee-jumping, a non-fiction description of someone's first jump, and an article warning about the risks of adventure sports.

Writing test

This test is **1 hour** and **15 minutes** long, including 15 minutes planning time. It consists of two writing tasks: Section A (30 marks) and Section B (20 marks, including 4 marks for spelling). The exam paper will tell you how long to spend on each – 30 minutes on Section A, 20 minutes on Section B.

Bear in mind what purpose and audience you are given for writing: for example, 'Write a speech for parents ... '. Plan your writing carefully using the format provided. Allow time to check your work at the end. Mark any changes clearly and neatly.

Shakespeare test

This test lasts **45 minutes** and requires knowledge of one Shakespeare play. It carries 18 marks. There is only one task set for each play. It will relate to two extracts, one from each of the longer extracts you have studied. You should focus on the extracts given, but if you know the whole play, it may help if you show that you understand the context of the extracts (what comes before and after them). Remember: in this section of the test you are being tested on your understanding, not your writing – although you need to write well enough for the examiner to understand you!

Fiction and non-fiction

1 Everything you read is either fiction or non-fiction.

- Fiction is writing that comes from the imagination, especially novels and stories.
- Non-fiction is based on fact, but it can include opinions and arguments.

2 All fiction and some non-fiction is literary, meaning that it gives us more than the bare facts and uses imaginative language,

- It uses well-chosen descriptive words, including adjectives and adverbs.
- It uses images – word pictures that make us imagine what is being described.

- It may tell a story, even if it is a true one.
- It aims to entertain.

3 Literary non-fiction includes:

Biography

During his three years at Berlin University, Marx was seldom in the lecture hall and often in debt.

(Francis Wheen, *Karl Marx*)

Autobiography

My friend, I am going to tell you the story of my life, as you wish; and if it were only the story of my life I think I would not tell it; for what is one man that he should make much of his winters, even when they bend him like a heavy snow?

(*Black Elk Speaks*, ed. John Neihardt)

Diaries

It's utterly impossible to build my life on a foundation of chaos, suffering and death. I see the world being slowly transformed into a wilderness. I hear the approaching thunder that, one day, will destroy us too, I feel the suffering of millions.

(*Anne Frank's Diary*)

Travel writing

Pack-ice might be described as a gigantic and interminable jigsaw puzzle devised by Nature. The parts of the puzzle in loose pack have floated slightly apart and become disarranged.

(Sir Ernest Shackleton, *South*)

Remember

Fiction is made up. Non-fiction is based on fact. Literary writing uses good descriptive words and images, may tell a story, and aims to entertain.

Work-out!

Copy and complete

```
                    fiction ──────▶  1 novels
                   ┌────────┐        2
  ┌──────────┐────▶
  │literature│
  └──────────┘────▶ ┌────────┐
        │           └────────┘─────▶  1
        ▼                             2 biography
  ┌──────────────────┐               3
  │ 1 description  2  │               4
  │ 3              4  │
  └──────────────────┘
```

2 mins

1 What are the two main kinds of fiction?
2 What is non-fiction based on?
3 What kind of non-fiction would these books be?
   a Pygmies and Pagodas
   b My Horrible Life
4 Which type of writing often tells a story?
5 What are 'images' in literary writing?

Question and model answer

Comment on how the following extract entertains. The author considers the perils of hiking in the USA.

It required only a little light reading in adventure books and almost no imagination to envision circumstances in which I would find myself caught in a tightening circle of hunger-emboldened wolves, staggering and shredding clothes under an onslaught of pincered fire ants, or dumbly transfixed by the sight of enlivened undergrowth advancing towards me, like a torpedo through water, before being bowled backwards by a sofa-sized boar with cold beady eyes, a piercing squeal, and a slaverous, chomping appetite for pink, plump, city-softened flesh.

(Bill Bryson, *A Walk in the Woods*)

1 The author invites us to laugh at his foolish fears. Despite the phrase 'almost no imagination', he is highly imaginative.

2 His fears of animals are exaggerated, as is the descriptive language he uses. He employs a device: taking three examples and making each in turn more extreme to build to a climax.

3 Adjectives like 'hunger-emboldened', and the phrases 'tightening circle' and 'onslaught', are colourfully dramatic. Calling the boar 'sofa-sized' amusingly relates it to ordinary indoor life; 'city-softened flesh' adds to the contrast. The torpedo simile is vivid, while the alliteration of 'before being bowled backwards' suggests the animal bursting out.

Comments

1 Immediately identifies the author's aim – to entertain – and his means of doing it.

2 Links the exaggerated content with the language and identifies how the structure works.

3 Focuses on descriptive phrases and their effect, and on sounds. Good use of terminology.

Now try this!

Bill Bryson later describes another risk. Comment on what makes this literary.

Imagine, if you will, lying in the dark alone in a little tent, nothing but a few microns of trembling nylon between you and the chill night air, listening to a 400-pound bear moving around your campsite. Imagine its quiet grunts and mysterious snufflings, the clatter of upended cookware and sounds of moist gnawings, the pad of its feet and the heaviness of its breath, the singing brush of its haunch along your tent side.

KS3 Bitesize English   7

Fact, opinion and bias

1 Facts: A fact **is something agreed to be true, and for which there is** evidence:

- Some parents smack children.
- Car batteries contain acid.

2 Opinions: An opinion **is a point of view or** judgement:

- Smacking children encourages violence.
- The speed limit should be raised on motorways.

3 Bias: Bias **is shown when a writer** presents facts **in a way that supports an opinion:**

- England played dazzlingly, coming close to scoring on several occasions. The Cup would have been ours had it not been for Germany's three very uninspired set-piece goals.

Score

Germany 3	England 0

4 Both fiction and non-fiction (see page 6) can contain facts, opinions and bias.

Fact, opinion and bias in different types of writing:

Fiction	May be based on fact (e.g. a historical novel); characters may express opinions (including the author's).
Non-fiction	Contains more facts than fiction does, but often contains opinions and may be biased.
'Leader' articles and editorials	Argue opinions.
Other news reporting	Can be biased, deliberately (e.g. to support a political party) or unconsciously: writers can be influenced by their views and feelings without realising it.

5 There are different types of bias:

- **Selection**: giving only some of the facts.
- **Exaggeration** or its opposite – understatement.
- **Emotive language**: manipulating our emotions by choice of words.
- **Interpretation**: what conclusions the writer reaches.

HELP!

Don't be tricked by phrases that disguise opinions as facts:
- *It's a well-known fact that …*
- *All the evidence shows that …*
- *Only a fool could doubt that …*

Remember

- Facts can be *proven*.
- Opinions can be *argued*.
- Bias *disguises* opinions as facts.

Copy and complete

facts → provable

opinions → [ ]

bias → [ ]

bias → unconscious

Disguises _____ as _____

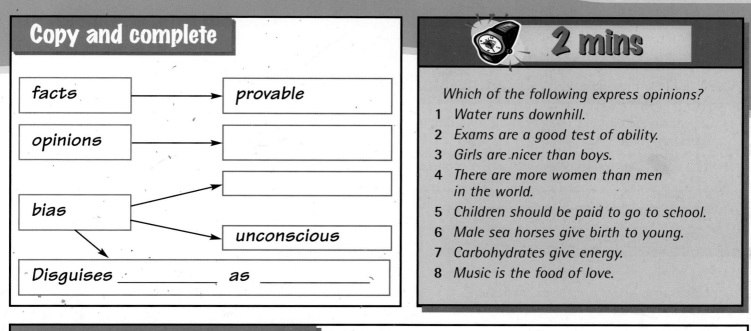

Which of the following express opinions?
1 *Water runs downhill.*
2 *Exams are a good test of ability.*
3 *Girls are nicer than boys.*
4 *There are more women than men in the world.*
5 *Children should be paid to go to school.*
6 *Male sea horses give birth to young.*
7 *Carbohydrates give energy.*
8 *Music is the food of love.*

Question and model answer

Explain how the following letter shows opinion bias.

Dear Sir,
I wish to draw your attention to the misuse of Broadmead shopping precinct by skateboarders. Gangs of these young hoodlums seem to lurk around corners lying in wait for innocent persons such as myself to appear. They terrorise young children and pensioners with their silly stunts. No one in their right mind could doubt that they are the greatest menace on our streets today.

Yours, Disgusted of Fishponds

The word 'misuse' expresses the writer's opinion. The words 'gangs', 'lurk' and 'hoodlums' are emotive, implying that the skateboarders are criminals or thugs. The mention of 'young children and pensioners' is also emotive, since we might have special sympathy for these groups. The reference to 'silly stunts' is dismissive, the alliteration emphasising this. The final sentence uses a popular technique of bias: suggesting that anyone who disagrees must be mad. It also tries to make readers feel that they and the writer are on the same side, against the skateboarders, by using the phrase 'our streets'. The claim itself is highly exaggerated. Finally, the writer is selective, ignoring the benefits of skateboarding.

Comment
This answer closely analyses the actual words used, even pointing out the use of alliteration (the repetition of sounds) for emphasis. It distinguishes between opinion and bias, and identifies three techniques of bias: emotive language, exaggeration and selection.

Now try this!

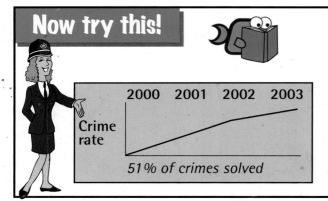

2000 2001 2002 2003

Crime rate

51% of crimes solved

Look at the graph and at the headlines based on the information in the graph.

| A Police solve most crimes |
| B Nearly half of all crimes unsolved |
| C Police catch more criminals than ever |
| D More criminals are escaping justice |
| E Crime increase rate going down |

Explain how each headline is biased. What two techniques of bias are used? (See list of types, opposite.)

Meaning and themes

1 The **meaning** of a text is what the writer **intends** to say. Its **themes** are the underlying ideas explored.

- The **basic** meaning of words can be found in a **dictionary**.
- You also need to **make sense** of the sentences.

- You may have to **read between the lines** for **implied** meanings.
- **Themes** relate to **overall** meaning.

2 To understand sentences, it helps to know how they are constructed.

- Sentences can be **questions** – *Who are you?* **commands** – *Get out!* or **exclamations** – *Not you again!* But most are **statements**.

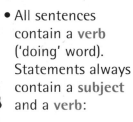

- All sentences contain a **verb** ('doing' word). Statements always contain a **subject** and a **verb**:

  The gorilla ate.

- You could add an **object** (the thing to which something is done):

  The gorilla ate a grape.

3 *Compound* and *complex* sentences are a little more complicated.

- **Compound sentences** join two simple ones:

  The gorilla ate a grape and went to sleep.

- **Complex sentences** include a **main clause** and one or more **subordinate clauses**:

  The gorilla, tiring of our chess game, ate a grape.

- Complex sentences are easier to follow if you **identify the main clause** – the bit that makes sense on its own (in green above).

4 An *implied* meaning is one which is hinted at:

- *Nobody kept Mr Big waiting – if they valued their health.*

Remember

You need to understand the words, the sentences, any extra implied meanings, and the overall themes.

5 Themes *are open to interpretation*.

- Different **readers** see different **ideas** in a piece of writing, or at least rank them differently. For example, you could see the **main theme** of *The Lord of the Rings* as good v. evil, greed v. self-sacrifice, or loyalty v. treachery.

Good

Evil

Copy and complete

| all sentences | — | subject + _____ |

| compound sentence | — | joins _____ _____ |

| complex sentence | — | main clause + _____ |

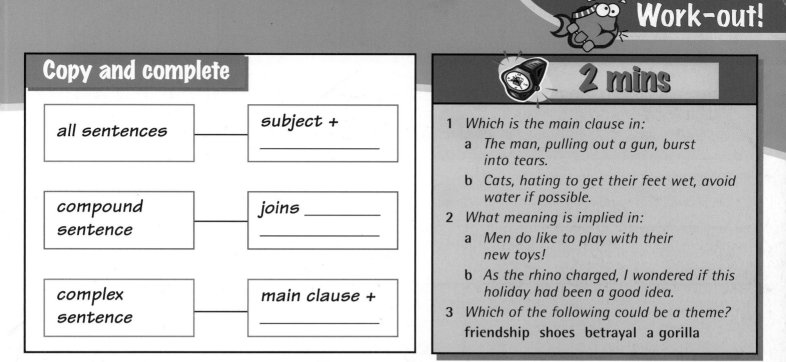

2 mins

1 Which is the main clause in:
   a The man, pulling out a gun, burst into tears.
   b Cats, hating to get their feet wet, avoid water if possible.
2 What meaning is implied in:
   a Men do like to play with their new toys!
   b As the rhino charged, I wondered if this holiday had been a good idea.
3 Which of the following could be a theme?
   friendship shoes betrayal a gorilla

Question and model answer

Read this passage about a wounded gunman, a boy and a baby, and answer the questions.

Inside the box was a sack. Sham leaned down and opened it up.

The baby was horrible. It was bright red and its blue eyes were all puffy and wet and red. When it saw us it started jerking and twitching and going redder and redder but it couldn't cry because it had a piece of tape over its mouth.

'That's my baby,' the gunman smiled. 'My little treasure.'

Sham reached down to pick it up but he shook his gun and said, 'Leave it!' fiercely.

'They need to be held,' said Sham. There was a funny moment. The man nodded sharply. Sham reached in and picked it up.

(Melvin Burgess, *The Baby and Fly Pie*)

1 **How does the narrator suggest the gunman's relationship with the baby?**
2 **Explain the 'funny moment'.**

1 The gunman is probably not the baby's father as he keeps it in cruel conditions. Its puffy eyes suggest that it has been crying a lot. He calls it his 'treasure' and reacts fiercely to Sham because it is valuable to him in some other way. Perhaps he has kidnapped it. He smiles at his own grim joke.

2 Sham must be used to babies as he knows they 'need to be held'. The 'moment' is while the gunman decides. He nods 'sharply' because he only reluctantly lets Sham touch the baby.

Comments

1 Good guess based on close reading. Notices the gunman's choice of words and his smile, and 'reads between the lines'. The kidnap suggestion is correct.

2 Uses evidence well, including short quotations. Notices the implied meaning in 'sharply'.

Now try this!

The passage above continues below. Comment on how it shows the narrator's attitude towards the baby, Sham and the man.

It was twitching and jerking in that horrible way as if it wasn't human at all. It was in a terrible mess — you know what babies are like. It had peed and crapped and that man hadn't done anything for it. It held out its arms and Sham cradled it against his chest. It looked awkward but he seemed to know what he was doing. At last it stopped twitching and began wriggling and nuzzling into Sham, making soft, choked little cries.

Values and emotions

1 Values are what people believe, especially about morality. They are connected to emotions.

- Values may be based on emotions:

  We should help suffering Third World children.

- They may give rise to emotions:

  No daughter of mine is going to marry a Martian!

2 Writers often express values and emotions, both in fiction and non-fiction.

- Values may be expressed in a neutral way:

  Shoplifting is wrong because it makes shops put up their prices so that honest people pay more.

- Or they can be expressed using emotive language (see pages 8–9):

  Shoplifters are parasites leeching off society.

3 A writer's choice of words can express values and emotions:

pensioners
geriatrics
old fogeys
strolling
tottering
shuffling

gripping
mindless
disgusting
adventure
blockbuster
orgy of violence

lads
youths
yobs
chatting
hanging about
lurking

4 Values and emotions are often expressed indirectly:

- through choice of words (as above)
- in fiction through characters, both in action and dialogue.

HELP!

In fiction, values and emotions expressed by characters are not necessarily those of the author.

Remember

Values are moral viewpoints. They can be based on emotion and can give rise to emotion. They are often expressed through emotive language.

Copy and complete

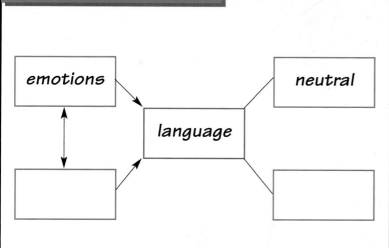

emotions → language ← neutral

2 mins

1 What kind of language is this?
   It is better to die on your feet than to live on your knees.
2 What value does this saying suggest?
3 What is the opposite of emotive language?
4 What kind of choice can a writer make to express values?
5 How might a writer express values in fiction?
6 What view is suggested by calling shoplifters 'parasites'?

Question and model answer

This extract is set after a nuclear war. The narrator, a teenage boy, has just rescued a girl from two boys chasing her for her food. She picks up an iron railing. Explain how the extract presents values and emotions.

I didn't know what she intended to do until she dropped her bag and lifted the spike above her head with both hands. I stood gaping till it was almost too late then flung myself at her, knocking her sideways and falling on top of her. The rail flew out of her hand and slithered away down the mound. The lad scrambled to his feet and tottered off holding his face.

I glanced at the long spike, then at the girl. She'd wriggled herself out from underneath me and was knocking dirt off her sleeve. She looked angry. I said, 'You wouldn't have done that would you, killed him, just like that?'

She glared at me, tight-lipped; straightening her dress. Then her features softened and she said, 'It's going to be us or them, you know.'

(Robert Swindells, *Brother in the Land*)

1 The use of the word 'lad' for the boy and the phrase 'scrambled to his feet and tottered off' suggest that he is no longer a threat, emphasising the girl's violence. The narrator thinks that killing is wrong. He cannot believe she would do this, so he stands 'gaping'.

2 We know she is angry from 'She looked angry' and her 'tight-lipped' glare. She is torn between gratitude and anger at being stopped. Her final statement shows her belief that any action is justified to ensure personal survival.

Comment

The answer identifies the contrasting values of the narrator and the girl, the girl's anger and the language that indicates it, and the fact that she justifies herself with a value statement. It also uses brief quotes to back up claims.

Now try this!

What values and emotions are shown in this account by a Native American present at Custer's Last Stand? How are they similar to those of the girl above?

He fell from his saddle, and I got off and beat him to death with my bow. I kept on beating him awhile after he was dead, and every time I hit him I said 'Hownh!'. I was mad, because I was thinking of the women and little children running down there, all scared and out of breath. These Wasichus* wanted it, and they came to get it, and we gave it to them.

(*Black Elk Speaks*, ed. John Neihardt)

*Non-native Americans

Setting and atmosphere

1 *Setting* means where a scene in a story or play takes place.

- The setting and how it is described create an **atmosphere**.
- The atmosphere prepares us for **events** and affects our reaction to them.

2 A *description* of the setting helps readers, or an audience, to imagine being there.

- Chapters of novels often start with a description of the setting. The author's **choice of details and words** create the right atmosphere for what is going to happen.
- The atmosphere helps us anticipate what is going to happen next in the story, for example, by building tension or creating a particular mood.
- The atmosphere can also affect our reactions to the events that take place.

3 Setting can also include:

- time of day
- time of year
- weather
- music
- sound effects
- lighting.

4 Think about what atmospheres you would associate with these two scenes.

- How might they be different at different times of day?
- What music or sound effects would you add to them in a film?
- What events do you expect to take place in these two settings?
- What other features can you think of to add to the atmosphere of these settings?

The setting alone is not enough to create atmosphere. Details and choice of words are important too.

Copy and complete

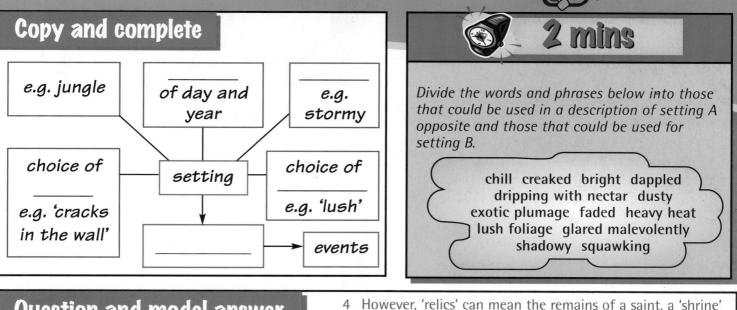

- e.g. jungle
- ___ of day and year
- e.g. stormy
- choice of ___ e.g. 'cracks in the wall'
- setting
- choice of ___ e.g. 'lush'
- ___
- events

2 mins

Divide the words and phrases below into those that could be used in a description of setting A opposite and those that could be used for setting B.

chill creaked bright dappled dripping with nectar dusty exotic plumage faded heavy heat lush foliage glared malevolently shadowy squawking

Question and model answer

Read the extract below carefully. Comment on how it uses setting to create atmosphere.

... the imperfect light entering by their narrow casements showed bedsteads of a hundred years old; chests in oak or walnut, looking, with their strange carvings of palm branches and cherubs' heads, like types of the Hebrew ark; rows of venerable* chairs, high-backed and narrow; stools still more antiquated, on whose cushioned tops were yet apparent traces of half-effaced embroideries, wrought by fingers that for two generations had been coffin-dust. All these relics gave to the third storey of Thornfield Hall the aspect of a home of the past — a shrine of memory. I liked the hush, the gloom, the quaintness of these retreats in the day; but I by no means coveted* a night's repose on one of those wide and heavy beds.

(Charlotte Brontë, *Jane Eyre*)

venerable: to be respected for their age
antiquated: ancient *coveted:* desired

1 This setting is cluttered with things from the past, such as the old bedsteads, the now unfashionable chairs and the even older stools. They create a sad feeling of lost times.

2 The idea that the hands that made the embroideries have long-since been 'coffin-dust' is a chilling reminder that all the people who made these things are dead.

3 The words 'relics' and 'shrine' also suggest death.

4 However, 'relics' can mean the remains of a saint, a 'shrine' is a place of worship, and the 'strange carvings' seem to be figures from the Bible. It is as if the past is worshipped here.

5 The atmosphere created is mysterious, but gloomy and even slightly menacing.

Comments

1 Describes the physical setting and the most obvious feeling it creates.
2 Interprets the physical detail and the emotional effect of the quoted phrase.
3 Focuses on the implied meaning (see page 10) of key words.
4 Offers a thoughtful personal interpretation of the words.
5 Clearly sums up the three main feelings created, using well-chosen words.

This is a level 7 answer. A level 5 would perhaps not show the same ability to focus on key words and phrases and interpret their implied meaning.

Now try this!

Choose a setting you know well. Describe it in a way that creates the right atmosphere for something frightening to take place there. Remember that you can use time and weather.

To write a level 7 answer, vary sentence length and structure; choose your words and details carefully (as in 'petered out' above); consider using an image (as in 'gaping windows' and 'burning brightly' above); and aim for a sense of development – not just a collection of random details.

Characterisation

1 **Characterisation** refers to the way in which a writer helps us to imagine what characters are like.

Look out for the following ways:
- **physical** appearance
- direct **description**
- **action** – what they do
- **dialogue** – what they say, how they say it, what others say about them
- a first person **narrator's thoughts** and **comments**.

2 **Physical appearance:** in real life we shouldn't judge by looks, but authors often make them match character.

- If we can picture characters they become more real.

Miss Dreadnought's steely hair was pinned in a bun tight enough to withstand a storm. The drawstrings of her mouth were pulled tight in a permanent pucker of disapproval. Her small eyes, darkly suspicious, peered into everything. She trusted no one.

3 **Direct description:** the most straightforward way of revealing a character.

- *Matty was a well-meaning boy, a little unsure of himself, but usually cheerful.*

4 **Action:** we can judge characters by what they do.

- *The man was unarmed and held a white flag. Vincent shot him dead without a thought.*

5 **Dialogue:** conversations are revealing both by **what is said** and **how it is said**.

> *'I – I could pay you ... just name an amount,' he offered desperately. She spun round. 'Do you think I'd accept your filthy money after what you've done?'*

6 **First person narration:** when the story is told by one character, their choice of words is revealing; they may also comment on other characters.

- *Shane was my least favourite kind of person – mouthy, self-satisfied and insensitive.*

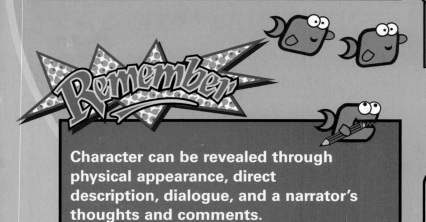

Remember

Character can be revealed through physical appearance, direct description, dialogue, and a narrator's thoughts and comments.

HELP!

Narrators may be unreliable – their account may be influenced by their own personality.

Work-out!

Copy and complete

physical _____

direct _____

character

Narrator's _____ and _____

Dialogue:
• what _____
• how _____
• what others _____

2 mins

1 What is the simplest way to reveal character?
2 What is 'first person' narration?
3 What might you guess about a narrator who says: 'Brian was chocolate-box handsome, disgustingly rich and undeservedly popular'?
4 What kind of text might include the phrases 'she sneered' and 'he answered softly'?
5 How can character be revealed without description or dialogue?

Question and model answer

Read the extract and answer the questions. Stanley is on his way to a boy's prison work camp. He is innocent.

Stanley and his parents had tried to pretend that he was just going away to camp for a while, just like rich kids do. When Stanley was younger he used to play with stuffed animals, and pretend the animals were at camp. Camp Fun and Games he called it. Sometimes he'd have them play soccer with a marble. Other times they'd run an obstacle course, or go bungee jumping off a table, tied to broken rubber bands. Now Stanley tried to pretend he was going to Camp Fun and Games. Maybe he'd make some friends, he thought. At least he'd get to swim in the lake.

(Louis Sachar, *Holes*)

1 **What does the phrase 'just like rich kids do' tell us about Stanley's home background?**
2 **What does the passage tell us about Stanley's relationship with his parents?**
3 **Find three features of Stanley's character and explain how they are suggested.**

1 Stanley comes from a fairly poor background.
2 Stanley must be close to them if they can share his fantasy. They must hate to think of him suffering.
3 Stanley plays alone, and he hopes to make friends at camp. This suggests that he has no friends. His continuing his game as fantasy shows that he avoids facing facts. His thoughts about friends and swimming show he is hopeful and ready to make the best of things.

Comment

These answers show an ability to look for 'implied meaning' (see page 10). Authors often reveal character in this way. In answer 3, the evidence is given clearly and concisely.

Now try this!

Read the first few pages of a novel and make notes on your first impressions of one character. Make a table for your notes using the headings opposite at the top of each column. (Ignore the 'First person narration' heading if the novel is in the third person.) You could photocopy the pages and colour-code your different sorts of character evidence.

Action and mood

1 Action refers to what real or fictional characters do. Mood refers to the general feeling created by what they do and say.

- **Action** is usually part of a **story**, and the author is concerned with its **pace** — the speed at which the action is revealed.

- **Mood** is closely connected to action. For example, **desperate** action involving danger will create a mood of **tension**.

2 In passages of action, verbs ('doing' words) are especially important:

- A verb alone can often express quite an exact idea. For example, you can **walk** to school or you can ...

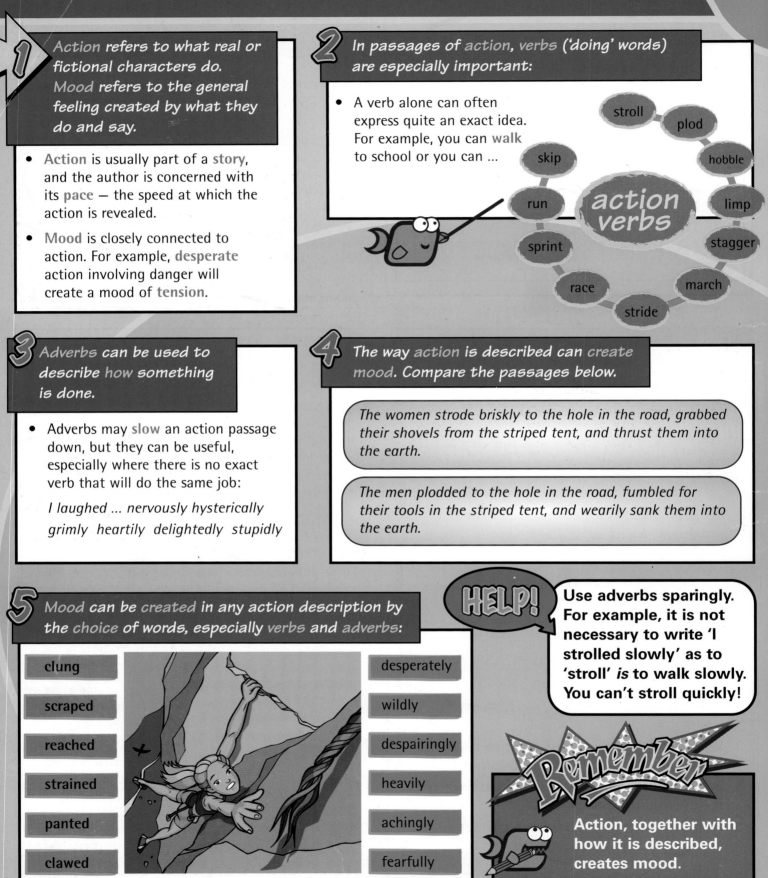

action verbs

stroll, plod, hobble, limp, stagger, march, stride, race, sprint, run, skip

3 Adverbs can be used to describe how something is done.

- Adverbs may **slow** an action passage down, but they can be useful, especially where there is no exact verb that will do the same job:

  I laughed ... nervously hysterically grimly heartily delightedly stupidly

4 The way action is described can create mood. Compare the passages below.

> The women strode briskly to the hole in the road, grabbed their shovels from the striped tent, and thrust them into the earth.

> The men plodded to the hole in the road, fumbled for their tools in the striped tent, and wearily sank them into the earth.

5 Mood can be created in any action description by the choice of words, especially verbs and adverbs:

clung, scraped, reached, strained, panted, clawed

desperately, wildly, despairingly, heavily, achingly, fearfully

HELP! Use adverbs sparingly. For example, it is not necessary to write 'I strolled slowly' as to 'stroll' *is* to walk slowly. You can't stroll quickly!

Remember

Action, together with how it is described, creates mood.

Copy and complete

```
┌──────────┐   ┌──────────────┐        ┌──────────┐
│  action  │──▶│     how      │───────▶│          │
└──────────┘   │  _____  │        └──────────┘
               └──────────────┘
                      │
               ┌──────────────┐
               │  Especially: │
               │  1 verbs     │
               │  2           │
               └──────────────┘
```

2 mins

1   Match the mood – horror or adventure:
   a   *Jabbing an elbow into his ribs, she flung herself from the window.*
   b   *The thing slithered into the gaping darkness.*
2   Identify which verbs in the lines above helped you to decide.
3   Rephrase the following to avoid adverbs.
   a   *She came into the room suddenly.*
   b   *A drunk walked awkwardly down the road.*

Question and model answer

Read the following extract. Then comment on its mood and how the author creates it.

The intense horror of nightmare came over me; I tried to draw back my arm, but the hand clung to it, and a most melancholy voice sobbed,

   'Let me in - let me in!'

   'Who are you?' I asked, struggling, meanwhile, to disengage myself.

   'Catherine Linton,' it replied shiveringly ... 'I'm come home: I'd lost my way on the moor!'

   As it spoke, I discerned, obscurely, a child's face looking through the window. Terror made me cruel; and, finding it useless to attempt shaking the creature off, I pulled its wrist on to the broken pane, and rubbed it to and fro till the blood ran down and soaked the bed-clothes: still it wailed, 'Let me in!'

(Emily Brontë, *Wuthering Heights*)

1   Brontë creates a mood of ghostly horror, 'the intense horror of 'nightmare', which is also sad and bleak, with the 'melancholy' sobbing of the child ghost. The word 'shiveringly' makes us think both of the freezing child and of the narrator's fear.
2   The words 'struggling' and 'disengage' suggest the narrator's frantic activity. The mood becomes more violent with the words 'Terror made me cruel'. The simple verbs 'pulled' and 'rubbed' show this bluntly, and the blood-soaked sheets make it more horrifying.

Comments

1   Shows a grasp of the overall mood, using an appropriate quote. Also shows an awareness that there is sadness as well as horror, reinforced by the double meaning of 'shivering'.

2   Focuses on the effect of the active verbs and draws accurate conclusions from them, particularly as to the subtle shift of mood from ghostliness to violence.

Now try this!

After the passage above, the narrator (Lockwood) cries out, bringing the owner of the house to the room. Read on and make notes on how the mood changes.

Heathcliff stood near the entrance, in his shirt and trousers, with a candle dripping over his fingers, and his face as white as the wall behind him. The first creak of the oak startled him like an electric shock; the light leaped from his hold to a distance of some feet, and his agitation was so extreme, that he could hardly pick it up.

Narrative viewpoint

1 Narrative viewpoint *means the point of view from which a story is told.*

- In **third person narrative** the author just tells the story: *Jack and Jill went up the hill.*
- In **first person narrative** a character tells it: *Jack and I went up the hill.*

2 In some *third person narrative* the author is 'all-knowing'.

- This kind of author can reveal all the **thoughts**, **feelings** and **actions** of the characters.
- But an author using **third person narrative** can still write from a particular **viewpoint**:

Jack was exasperated. Why was Jill always worrying about water?

Or ... *Jill sighed. That Jack! If it was left to him, they'd die of thirst.*

3 A *first person narrator* may be the main *character or a minor one.*

- A main character narrator is very involved in the story:

I'm Jill, and I once lived in a house below a hill.

- A minor character is less involved, and may recount parts of the story second-hand:

One day a lad staggered in with a terrible head injury. Said his name was Jack and did I have any brown paper. I asked him what had happened. 'Well,' he said ...

4 Sometimes a story is told by a *variety of methods,* such as using letters between characters to tell the story:

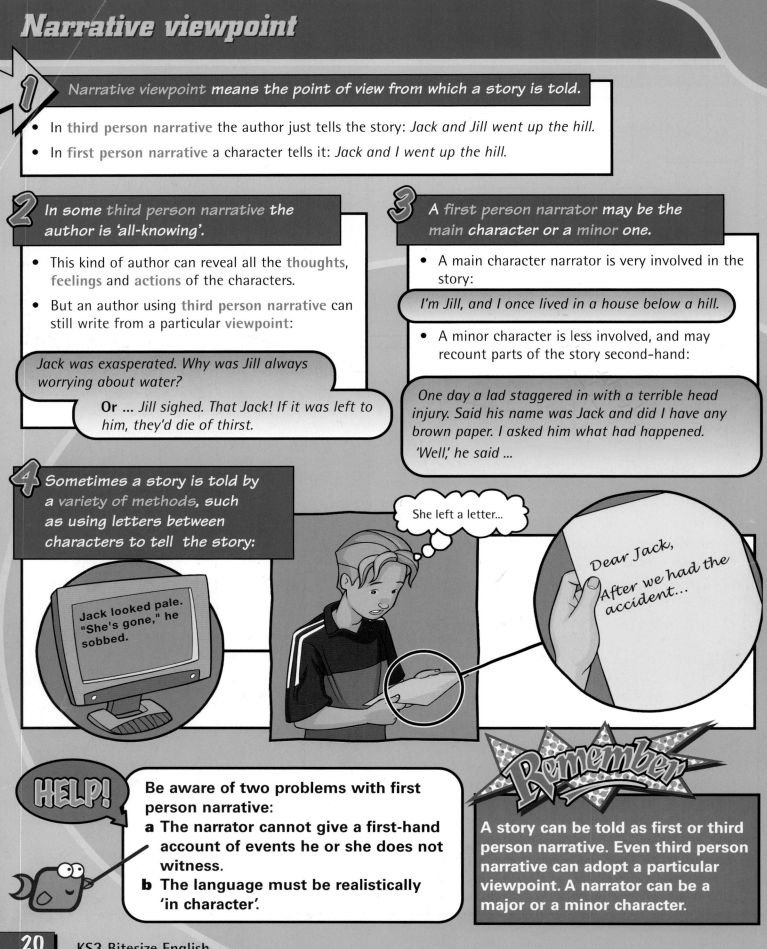

Jack looked pale. "She's gone," he sobbed.

She left a letter...

Dear Jack, After we had the accident...

HELP! Be aware of two problems with first person narrative:
- **a** The narrator cannot give a first-hand account of events he or she does not witness.
- **b** The language must be realistically 'in character'.

Remember

A story can be told as first or third person narrative. Even third person narrative can adopt a particular viewpoint. A narrator can be a major or a minor character.

Copy and complete

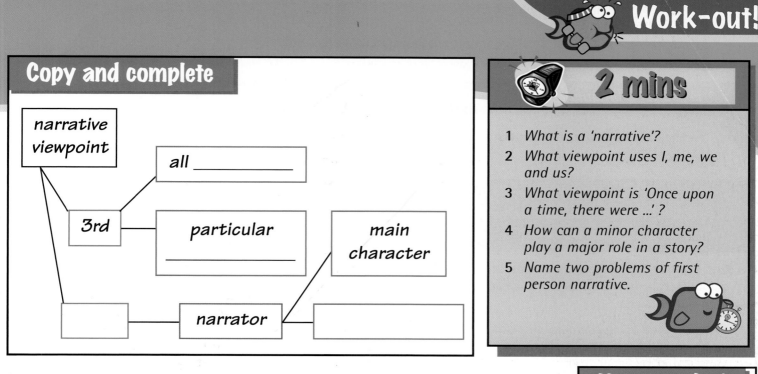

narrative viewpoint

all _____

3rd

particular _____

main character

narrator

1 What is a 'narrative'?
2 What viewpoint uses I, me, we and us?
3 What viewpoint is 'Once upon a time, there were ...' ?
4 How can a minor character play a major role in a story?
5 Name two problems of first person narrative.

Question and model answer

Read the following extract and answer the questions.

Good old Vince. Mum's boyfriend. You should see him. I mean, Mum's no Kylie Minogue – but Vincent. He's about fifty for a start, and he's one of these old dudes that wear cool gear and try to act young and it doesn't work because they've got grey hair and fat bellies and they just make themselves pathetic. And as if that's not enough, Vince likes his ale. I suppose Dad must've been a bit of a bastard in his way, but at least he wasn't a boozer. You should see the state Vincent's in when he and Mum come home from the club. He's got this very loud laugh – laughing at nothing, if you know what I mean – and he stands there with his arm round Mum, slurring his words as he tells me to call him Dad. Dad. I wouldn't call that fat pillock Dad if he was the last guy on earth.

(Robert Swindells, *Stone Cold*)

1 **With whom does the narrator compare Vincent, and how?**
2 **Identify two phrases that show the narrator's contempt for Vincent.**
3 **What do the phrase 'Good old Vince' and the final sentence suggest?**

1 The narrator compares him with his father, who at least wasn't a drunk like Vincent.

2 'pathetic', 'fat pillock'.

3 'Good old Vince' suggests bitter irony, or sarcasm: the narrator doesn't really feel affection for Vincent. The closing sentence suggests loyalty to his own father, and disgust at the idea of being related to Vincent - which may influence his judgement of Vincent.

Comment

The answers address the exact questions. They show an ability to look at the whole extract as well as individual phrases. The final answer shows a grasp of the fact that the narrator may not be speaking literally, and may not be objective. This makes it a level 7 answer.

Now try this!

Comment on the narrative viewpoint used below.

I trudged down the corridor towards the classroom used for detention. Everyone else had gone home. This was so unfair! I wouldn't get back till 6.30 at least, and then I'd miss 'The Simpsons'. As I rounded the corner a fleeting blue-clad figure fled into Room E37. My own entry was greeted by groans.

'That's enough!' I snapped. 'Get on with your detention work!'

Persuasive language

1

Persuasive language is used in *political speeches, leaflets, advertising* **and** *essays.*

- The art of using words to persuade is called **rhetoric**.

- The methods used in rhetoric are called **rhetorical devices**.

2 Rhetorical devices include:

- **Anticlimax** often ridicules: *They established committees, conducted in-depth research, and then did nothing.*

- **Climax** builds up to the most important point: *Smoking gives you bad breath, wastes your money, and seriously damages your health.*

- **Contrast**: *Leave the dark night of slavery for the new dawn of freedom.*

- **Emotive language**: *The road will rip up flowery meadows and leave a jagged scar.*

- **Exaggeration**: *My phone hasn't stopped ringing!*

- **Including the audience**: *We don't want drug dealers outside our schools.*

- **Irony** – saying the opposite of what is meant, in ridicule: *I'm sure the fox appreciates that hunting is a noble tradition.*

- **Quotations** to add authority (see opposite).

- **Repetition** – often used in threes: *Say no to crime, no to violence, and no to injustice.*

- **Rhetorical questions**, expecting no answer: *Has the world gone mad?*

- **Understatement**: *Starting a nuclear war by accident might prove embarrassing.*

3 See how Martin Luther King used some of these in 1963:

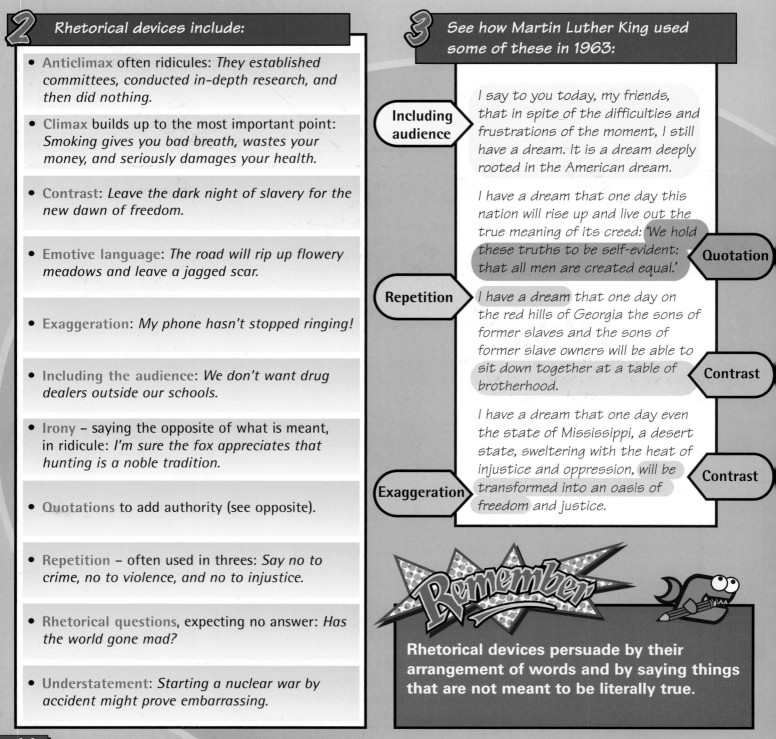

Including audience
I say to you today, my friends, that in spite of the difficulties and frustrations of the moment, I still have a dream. It is a dream deeply rooted in the American dream.

I have a dream that one day this nation will rise up and live out the true meaning of its creed: 'We hold these truths to be self-evident: that all men are created equal.' **Quotation**

Repetition I have a dream that one day on the red hills of Georgia the sons of former slaves and the sons of former slave owners will be able to sit down together at a table of brotherhood. **Contrast**

I have a dream that one day even the state of Mississippi, a desert state, sweltering with the heat of injustice and oppression, will be transformed into an oasis of freedom and justice. **Contrast**

Exaggeration

Remember

Rhetorical devices persuade by their arrangement of words and by saying things that are not meant to be literally true.

Copy and complete

Rhetorical questions don't expect _____ .

The opposite of exaggeration is _____ .

Irony says the opposite of _____ .

Repetition is often used in _____ .

Climax builds up to _____ .

2 mins

What devices are used here?
1 Are you a complete idiot?
2 War is cruel, war is stupid, war is wasteful.
3 I came, I saw, I conquered.
4 I have seen the blood of murdered babies ...
5 Blowing up your school is rather naughty.
6 A delicate flower growing on a dungheap ...

Question and model answer

Identify how the following passage sets out to persuade.

On a typical morning in any pretty English village, a solid line of commuter cars stretches as far as the eye can see. The delicate scent of roses is swamped by the poisonous stench of exhaust fumes. Is this progress? Of course, I'm not suggesting we should do anything as inconvenient as catching a bus to work. After all, global warming caused by vehicle pollution will only cause species extinction, the spread of tropical diseases, and massive climate change leading to the death of millions by slow starvation – minor inconveniences compared with queuing for a bus!

1 The passage paints a picture of the 'pretty English village', exaggeratedly filled with a 'solid line of cars stretching as far as the eye can see'. The idea of the dream village spoiled is emotive, as is the contrast between the scent of roses and the 'poisonous stench'.

2 The writer asks rhetorically 'Is this progress?', then ironically pretends that it would be too much for people to catch buses. The irony continues with the use of climax (building up to 'the death of millions') and understatement - 'only ...' and 'minor inconveniences'. The emotive 'slow starvation' is ironically contrasted with queuing for a bus.

Comment

The answer identifies the devices and shows how they are used to create the overall effect. It shows an awareness that devices can be combined, as in climax with understatement.

Now try this!

Read the continuation of the piece above, and comment on how it seeks to develop the persuasion begun above.

We have a simple choice: change our lifestyle or see life as we know it destroyed. World governments carefully considered this choice at Kyoto, made moving speeches, passed stern resolutions – then gave up and went home. If you want air we can breathe, if you want birdsong at dawn, if you want a planet we can inhabit, say no to cars!

Tone

1 *Tone refers to the style of language used by the writer to establish a particular relationship with the reader.*

For example, you would use a different tone to write:

- an apology to your head teacher
- a seaside postcard to a friend
- a complaint to the bank
- a letter of sympathy.

2 *Similarly, you would expect a different tone in:*

- a horror story
- a magazine article aimed at fans of a boy band
- an advert for expensive chocolates
- an entertaining holiday account
- an obituary (about someone who has just died).

3 *A writer's choice of tone is influenced by:*

- the **purpose** of the writing – for example, to **entertain**
- the **audience** it is aimed at – for example, **teenage fans**.

In focus WAYNE

You're probably all dying to know what yummy Wayne gets up to in in his spare time. Well, get this, readers....

4 *One aspect of tone, influenced by purpose and audience, is the level of formality used:*

It has come to my notice that some students have been stealing from the staff.

- **Formal** language is serious standard English.

Now, I've heard that some of you teachers have been nicking stuff off the kids.

- **Informal** language is more familiar and may include slang.

HELP! **Still in doubt about what 'standard English' is? It's the kind used by a BBC newsreader or in a serious newspaper so that a wide audience can understand. It contains no slang or dialect (see page 48), but it can be spoken in any accent.**

Remember

A writer's tone is all about the relationship he or she wants with the reader.

Copy and complete

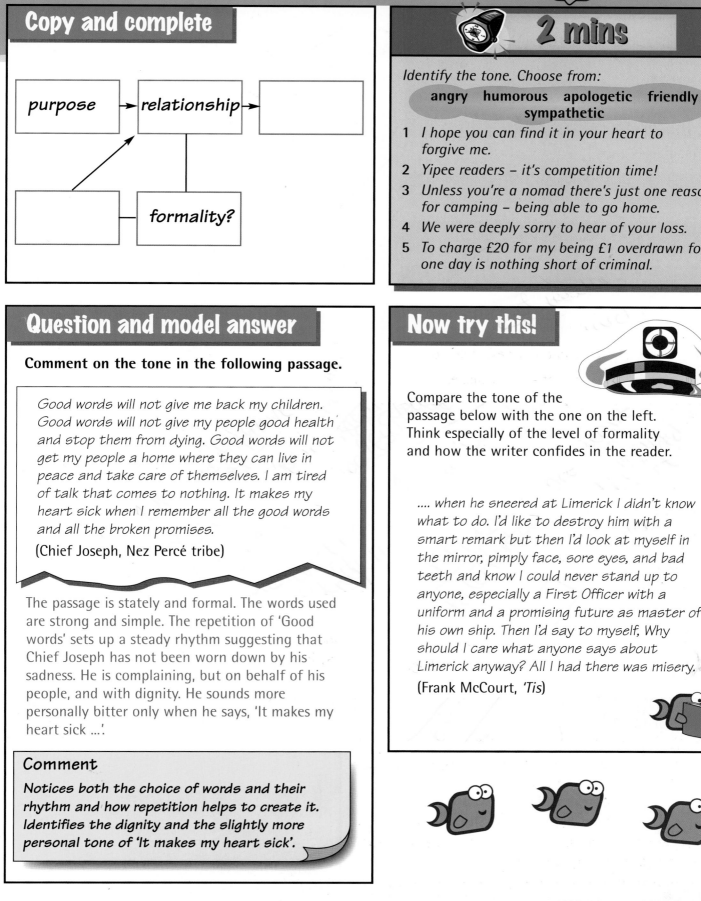

```
purpose  →  relationship  →  [        ]
                   ↑      
             [        ] — formality?
```

 **2 mins**

Identify the tone. Choose from:

**angry humorous apologetic friendly
sympathetic**

1 I hope you can find it in your heart to forgive me.
2 Yipee readers – it's competition time!
3 Unless you're a nomad there's just one reason for camping – being able to go home.
4 We were deeply sorry to hear of your loss.
5 To charge £20 for my being £1 overdrawn for one day is nothing short of criminal.

Question and model answer

Comment on the tone in the following passage.

Good words will not give me back my children. Good words will not give my people good health and stop them from dying. Good words will not get my people a home where they can live in peace and take care of themselves. I am tired of talk that comes to nothing. It makes my heart sick when I remember all the good words and all the broken promises.

(Chief Joseph, Nez Percé tribe)

The passage is stately and formal. The words used are strong and simple. The repetition of 'Good words' sets up a steady rhythm suggesting that Chief Joseph has not been worn down by his sadness. He is complaining, but on behalf of his people, and with dignity. He sounds more personally bitter only when he says, 'It makes my heart sick ...'.

Comment

Notices both the choice of words and their rhythm and how repetition helps to create it. Identifies the dignity and the slightly more personal tone of 'It makes my heart sick'.

Now try this!

Compare the tone of the passage below with the one on the left. Think especially of the level of formality and how the writer confides in the reader.

.... when he sneered at Limerick I didn't know what to do. I'd like to destroy him with a smart remark but then I'd look at myself in the mirror, pimply face, sore eyes, and bad teeth and know I could never stand up to anyone, especially a First Officer with a uniform and a promising future as master of his own ship. Then I'd say to myself, Why should I care what anyone says about Limerick anyway? All I had there was misery.

(Frank McCourt, 'Tis)

Figurative language

1 Figurative language *uses* figures of speech – expressions that create word pictures to describe a thing or a situation more vividly.

The main ones are:

- simile
- metaphor
- personification
- analogy.

3 Metaphors *compare things to something else, without using as or like.*

- *Revenge is a dish best eaten cold.*
- *We must brave the hungry beast of war.*

5 An analogy *is an* explanation of *something by comparing it with something different:*

- *Education is like a house: it needs secure foundations.*
- *Inviting Cynthia to your wedding is like asking the Big Bad Wolf to babysit.*

2 Similes *use* like *or* as, *making the comparison obvious:*

- *She's* like *a diamond shining in the dirt.*
- *He's* as *scratchy* as *a bramble bush.*

4 Personification *is a kind of metaphor which describes an* abstract *thing as a* person:

- *The UK economy has caught a nasty cold.*
- *When the wolf is at the door, love flies out the window.*

 **HELP!**

Figures of speech make things more vivid, but they also add to the overall mood of a piece of writing (see page 18).

 **Remember**

Figures of speech, or images, paint vivid pictures, often of abstract things. The main types are simile (using 'like' or 'as'), metaphor, personification and analogy.

Copy and complete

simile		uses like or _____
		describes x as if y
personification		
		explains _____

Identify these figures of speech:

1 It sank like a stone.
2 Fear prodded me into action.
3 It's like untying a knot – you have to see how it was tied.
4 My single rocketed to Number One.
5 I'm happy as a sand-boy.
6 The Arctic winter is pitiless.
7 She was catapulted to stardom.

Question and model answer

Comment on how figurative language is used below.

Diving your first 'sump' – an underwater cave passage – is like stepping off a cliff blindfolded having been promised a soft landing: it's hard to believe you'll survive. You crouch, icy fingers of water probing your wet suit, breathe deeply to calm the drumbeat of your heart, grasp a rope disappearing into soupy water, fill your lungs, and plunge. A few tugs and you burst like a flying fish into airspace on the far side. Exhilarated and relieved, you wonder why you worried, until it hits you: there's only one way out – back through the sump!

The passage helps readers to imagine the experience. It begins with an analogy to give an idea of the diver's doubts. Using the word 'you' to involve the reader, it appeals to the senses: touch – the personification of 'icy fingers probing', as if the water were human; hearing – the metaphor of the heart pounding like a drum; and sight – the metaphor of the water 'soupy' with mud. The 'flying fish' simile suggests how quickly the diver emerges. Finally, 'until it hits you' contains another metaphor, expressing the sudden and slightly unwelcome realisation.

Comment

This is a level 7 or 8 answer as it explains why the writer uses figurative language, identifies the types used and explains how each works, identifies the appeal to the senses, and comments on how the pronoun 'you' supplements this language.

Now try this!

Write a paragraph of your own describing the diving experience but using your own figurative language. Use the passage as a framework, replacing a metaphor with a metaphor of your own, a simile with a simile, and so on. Alternatively, write about the experience shown on the right – or one of your own.

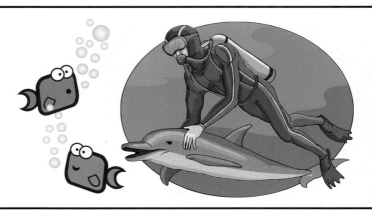

Structure

1 **A good piece of writing is structured:**

- At the very least it has a **beginning**, a **middle** and an **end**.
- Other **turning points** may be **signalled** by **link words** and **phrases**.

2 **To understand structure, look at the piece as a whole.**

- The **beginning** will **introduce** the subject, aiming to catch the reader's **interest** and **hinting at what is to come**.
- The **middle** part presents the **main ideas**, often in **stages**, or with several **twists** of argument.
- The **end** concludes, perhaps **summing up** or making a **final point**, which may be **humorous** or somehow point towards the **future**.

3 **Link words and phrases are signals to the reader:**

- **However**: signals a contradiction or qualification of what has just been said.
- **Yet, But**: like 'However' but more immediate and less formal.
- **Despite this, Nevertheless, Nonetheless**: signal a stronger contradiction.
- **Similarly, Likewise, In the same way**: signal a point echoing a previous one.
- **Moreover, Furthermore, What's more, In addition**: signal an additional point.
- **Therefore, Consequently, As a result**: signal cause and effect.
- **On the other hand**: signals a different view or angle balancing the first.
- **Certainly**: acknowledging a fact but preparing for a contradiction.

4 **A writer can guide us through a progression of ideas.**

For example, an article on fitness:

> Introduction: do we need to be fit?

> Arguments against and in favour.

> How diet relates to this.

> The social angle – unfit people need more health care.

> Warning against overdoing exercise.

> Conclusion: get fit and eat healthy food and you'll benefit.

HELP!

Paragraphs are used to arrange ideas. A new paragraph often introduces a new idea.

Remember

Good writing is structured. Link words and phrases tell the reader what to expect.

Work-out!

Copy and complete

beginning	introduces, catches _____, hints at _____
_____	contains main _____
_____	con_____

2 mins

1 What should the opening catch?
2 What are paragraphs for?
3 What do link words and phrases do?
4 What link word signals a contradiction or qualification?
5 Name a link word signalling cause and effect.

Question and model answer

The passage below is based on the first two points in the flow chart opposite. Identify the four link words and explain how they are used.

> How fit are you? We now eat more, and exercise less, than ever before. But if we don't need to hunt animals or escape from them, do we need to be fit?
>
> Certainly, we can survive without being fit. Vehicles take us to school and work, and machines do our chores. Yet medical evidence shows that aerobic exercise has many benefits. It increases alertness, produces chemicals that make us happier, and boosts our immune system. Moreover, keeping slim reduces strain on the heart.

1 'But' (if we ...) signals a possible argument against the need for fitness.
2 'Certainly' admits that there could be some truth in the idea that we don't need to be fit.
3 'Yet' (medical evidence ...) signals a contradiction of the anti-fitness argument.
4 'Moreover' announces an added benefit.

Comment

The answer correctly identifies the link words and shows how they work with the ideas, joining them together and guiding the reader through them.

Now try this!

Comment on how link words and phrases support structure in the remainder of the article.

Similarly, eating a healthy diet with plenty of fruit and vegetables and limited fat and sugar has beneficial effects.

Despite this, many people get no exercise and eat junk food. As a result, the health services are overloaded. On the other hand, overdoing it is bad too. Exercising unprepared can lead to muscle strain, or even a heart attack for older people.

In general, however, the message is clear. Get regular exercise and eat healthy food, and you'll be happier and live longer. Conversely, if you're a couch potato and live on chips and chocs, you'll pay the price.

Nouns and pronouns

1 **Nouns** *are the words for things. There are four types:*

- **Concrete** nouns identify **things** experienced through the senses – things you can see, hear, touch, smell or taste: *rainbow, song, table, coffee, treacle.*

- **Abstract** nouns identify **ideas** and **emotions**: *luck, love, peace, joy, education.*

- **Collective** nouns identify groups of things: *herd, family, flock.*

- **Proper** nouns are the names for individual people, places, organisations, ships, etc., and always start with a capital: *Rashid, Bradford, Boyzone, HMS Endurance.*

2 **Pronouns** *replace nouns in sentences to avoid repeating them. The main types are:*

- **Personal** pronouns are for people or things. As the **subject** of a sentence they are: *I, you, he, she, one, it, we, they.* As the **object** some are different: *me, him, her, us, them.*

- **Reflexive** pronouns: *myself, yourself, himself, itself, ourselves, yourselves, themselves.*

- **Possessive** pronouns show ownership: *my, your, his, her, its, our, their.* Some change when including the thing owned: *mine, yours, hers, theirs.*

- **Relative** pronouns connect one clause to another: *who, whose, which, that – Donna, who doesn't smoke, opened a window.*

- **Indefinite** pronouns refer to people or things in general: *some, many, anything, nobody, none,* etc. – *Some like it hot.*

3 *Choice of noun is important.*

- **Abstract** nouns can give a sense of importance (*poverty* and *violence*), but **concrete** nouns can feel more immediate (*slums* and *bullets*).

- **Nouns** meaning **almost** the same thing can have subtly different meanings, which can affect **mood** and **tone**.

4 *Pronouns can influence tone, especially in persuasive writing:*

- **I** *hate to see* **my** *money wasted on rubbish.* (**Personal**)

- **You** *should read this carefully.* (**Addressing reader directly**)

- **We** *all make mistakes.* (**Including the reader**)

- **One** *hopes this problem is now solved.* (**Formal, impersonal**)

Remember

Nouns (concrete, abstract, collective, proper) are words for things. Pronouns (personal, reflexive, possessive, relative, indefinite) replace nouns in sentences.

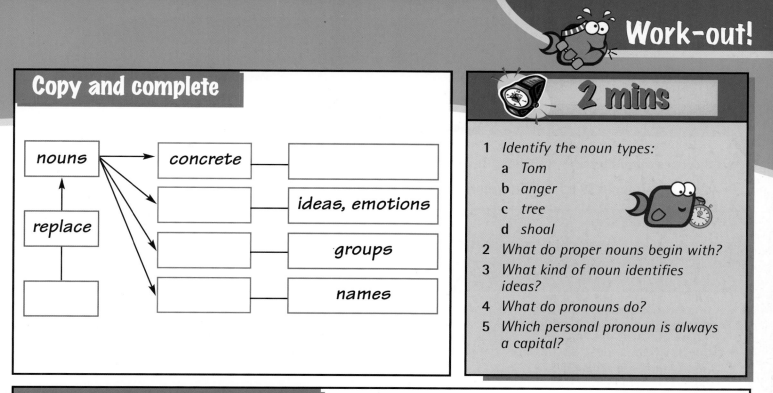

Copy and complete

nouns → concrete

replace → nouns

concrete
ideas, emotions
groups
names

2 mins

1 Identify the noun types:
 a Tom
 b anger
 c tree
 d shoal
2 What do proper nouns begin with?
3 What kind of noun identifies ideas?
4 What do pronouns do?
5 Which personal pronoun is always a capital?

Question and model answer

Read this passage and answer the questions.

African countries are struggling to replace shackles and shacks with freedom and equality. Yet game reserves present a moral dilemma. I've seen a wonderful range of wildlife on the Serengeti reserve – rhino, antelope, giraffe, wildebeest, warthog, impala, lions, to name a few. Traditionally this land was open to all, but one cannot allow any Tom, Dick or Harry to wander over it with a rifle if one is to preserve this diversity. We all want to help the poor man to feed his children, but we also want to preserve wildlife.

1 How are concrete and abstract nouns used in the first sentences?
2 How are animal names and other names used?
3 Comment on the use of the pronouns I, one, we.

1 The sentence contrasts two concrete nouns, 'shackles and shacks', with two abstract nouns, 'freedom and equality'. The concrete nouns here stand for abstract ideas: 'shackles' for slavery or injustice, and 'shacks' for poverty. The abstract nouns suggest ideals.
2 The list of animals suggests the great variety of wildlife. 'Serengeti' identifies the reserve discussed, but the names Tom, Dick and Harry stand for 'any ordinary person'.
3 'I've seen' asserts personal experience. The phrases 'one cannot allow' and 'if one is' give the claim a tone of authority. The repeated 'we' invites us to identify with the writer.

Comment
The answers show a grasp of the different types of noun and pronoun, an ability to identify them, and an awareness of what effect the writer aims for in using them.

Now try this!
Look up the nouns in the illustration opposite in a good dictionary. Consider how their meanings are subtly different and how you would use each one.

Adjectives

1 Adjectives *provide* information *about* nouns.

- Adjectives of **quality** tell you what a thing is like: *good dog, pink towel, careful driver.*
- Adjectives of **quantity** tell you **how many** or **how much**: *two cats, some tea, few boys.*

2 Comparatives *and* superlatives *make* comparisons.

- **Comparatives:** *kinder, tastier, better, worse, more hopeful* (not *hopefuller*).
- **Superlatives:** *kindest, tastiest, best, worst, most hopeful* (not *hopefullest*).

3 Nouns *and* verbs *can often be used as* adjectives.

- **Nouns:** *door stop, coat hook, feather bed.*
- **Verbs:** *hunting party, fishing trip, waiting game.*

4 *Careful choice of adjectives can make a description more vivid or accurate:*

huge head

pale green skin

several mouths

wobbly eyes

long, skinny arms

HELP!

Adjectives describe nouns; adverbs are used with verbs.

Remember

Adjectives give information about nouns; comparatives (mostly ending in *-er*) and superlatives (mostly ending in *-est*) make comparisons; nouns and verbs can be used as adjectives. Adjectives make descriptions more vivid or accurate.

Copy and complete

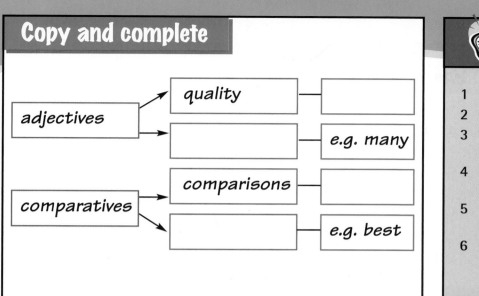

adjectives → quality → [ ]

→ [ ] → e.g. many

comparatives → comparisons → [ ]

→ [ ] → e.g. best

1 What do adjectives provide?
2 What two main kinds are there?
3 What are **bigger** and **smaller** examples of?
4 What are **easiest** and **stupidest** examples of?
5 What parts of speech do adjectives describe?
6 What other two parts of speech can be used as adjectives?

Question and model answer

How do adjectives make the description below more vivid?

As I stepped down onto the dusty red soil I felt excited but a little anxious. After several minutes, three strange and rather fearsome creatures appeared over the rocky horizon – my first Martians. They had huge heads relative to their bodies, wobbly eyes on delicate stalks, and long, skinny arms with little hands that clutched what looked like oversized fountain pens. Their pale green skin glowed luminously. Each had several mouths, all limp, rubbery in appearance, and oddly sinister.

We see the setting in 'dusty red' and 'rocky', and get a fairly exact idea of the narrator's feelings in 'excited but a little anxious'. A sense of time passing is given in 'several minutes'. The narrator's response is shown by the phrase 'strange and rather fearsome'. The adjectives used for the Martians make them seem alien (especially their huge heads and odd mouths), almost comical ('wobbly', 'skinny', 'little'), yet threatening ('sinister').

Comment

The answer picks out the details of the setting and the Martians, and notes that the narrator's feelings are given in some detail. It spots the viewpoint contained in 'strange and rather fearsome' and the different impressions made by the other adjectives.

Now try this!

Read the opening of a novel. Jot down each adjective that occurs, together with the noun it describes, until you have at least ten adjectives. Beside each phrase, comment on how the adjective makes the description more vivid or accurate.

Reading the SATs passages

1
You have to answer questions on *three passages* in your SATs Reading paper.

- The exam lasts 75 minutes. Of this, 15 minutes is for reading, but you can re-read the passages, or parts of them, if necessary.

- The passages will be related in **subject** (what they're about) but different in **type** – fiction and non-fiction, literary and non-literary.

2
You will be asked *questions* in different formats.

- These will be aimed at **word**, **sentence** and **text level**. For example, you may be asked about the language of one paragraph, how a particular sentence builds up tension, or the overall effect of the passage.

- Questions will take a **variety of forms**, for example, completing a table or tick box. Just do what is asked.

- Write clearly, but remember that you're being tested on **reading ability**, not writing.

3
Questions will test *different sorts of reading ability:*

- reading for **meaning**
- finding **information**
- **interpreting** what you read
- understanding **structure**
- appreciating how **language** is used
- identifying the writer's **viewpoint** and **purpose**
- understanding the text's **historical** and **literary context**.

4
Try this *approach*:

Glance at all the passages to see roughly what they're about. You should see a **connection**. If not, don't worry.

Skim the first passage quickly to get more of an idea of what the whole passage is about, and of its structure. Look especially at paragraph beginnings.

Then **read** the first passage **closely**. Underline key words or phrases if that helps.

Notice **tone** and **mood**, **setting** (if any) and how it affects **atmosphere**, **viewpoint**, and how **language** is used – choice of words, imagery, etc.

Ask yourself how the writer's **purpose** and **audience** determine the **style**.

Skim and **closely read** the other passages. You'll appreciate their features more if you mentally **compare** the passages. Some questions may include comparison.

Remember

You have to answer a variety of questions on three passages related in subject but different in type. Questions relate to different sorts of reading ability. Use the 'Glance, Skim, Closely Read' approach, looking out for literary features. Consider purpose and audience.

Copy and complete

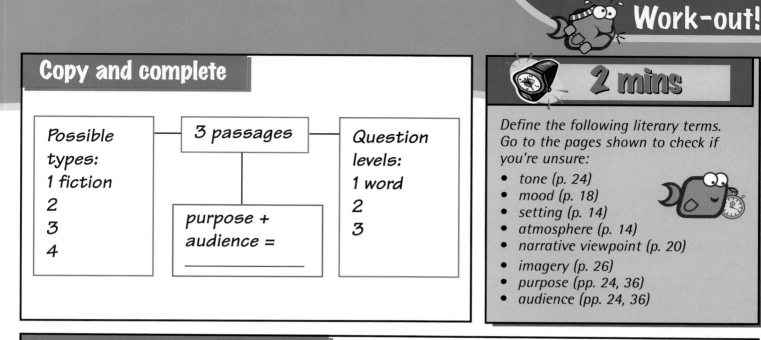

Possible types:
1 fiction
2
3
4

— 3 passages —

purpose + audience = _____

Question levels:
1 word
2
3

2 mins

Define the following literary terms. Go to the pages shown to check if you're unsure:

- tone (p. 24)
- mood (p. 18)
- setting (p. 14)
- atmosphere (p. 14)
- narrative viewpoint (p. 20)
- imagery (p. 26)
- purpose (pp. 24, 36)
- audience (pp. 24, 36)

Question and model answer

This is not a typical SATs question, but will help you focus on the kinds of literary feature you might find.

What features are likely to be targeted in questions on the following:

1 A stone-floored passage, chill and inky beyond my feeble torch. Spiders scuttled away ...

2 Waves of sorrow swept over her, sinking her hope like a raft in a storm.

3 Brad clung desperately to the log as it swung in the boiling current ...

4 George felt rebellious. Why should he obey orders? He would surprise them all!

5 Say no to poverty, say no to sickness, say no to endless wars and conflict!

6 So you've dashed out to the summer sales and bought a skimpy new top? Big mistake.

7 The G17X is not for everyone. Only the discerning buyer will appreciate ...

1 Setting and atmosphere.

2 Imagery.

3 Mood – tension.

4 Narrative viewpoint – the story is in the third person but from George's viewpoint.

5 Rhetorical devices – used in persuasive writing.

6 Tone – here it is friendly and informal.

7 Purpose and audience – here, to sell something expensive to people who pride themselves on their wealth and good judgement.

Now try this!

What features are likely to be targeted in questions on the following:

1 I am outraged at the suggestion that I owe you anything at all. How dare you ...

2 I trudged heavily along, weighed down by the burden of my thoughts.

3 I'm Sue, and this is my story. I never used to think much ...

4 If it is your first time on a skateboard, be very careful to ...

5 The leafy dell in which we spread our picnic was lit with dappled sunlight ...

6 The wall ballooned alarmingly, then burst like a lanced boil.

7 We risk the ruin of our rural heritage by urban sprawl.

Purpose and audience

1 When you write, focus on your *purpose* and your intended *audience*.

- Your writing **purpose** means the **effect** you want to achieve.

- Your **audience** is who you are aiming your writing at. Your exam answers will be read by the examiners, but you may be asked to imagine a special audience – for example, teachers thinking of buying a new Shakespeare video.

- Your **purpose** and **audience** should determine your writing's **content** (what's in it) and **style** (how it's written).

2 *Audiences* for writing *vary in* many ways.

- **Age:** for example, teenagers or pensioners.

- **Specialisation:** for example, readers of a skateboard magazine.

- **Educational:** *The Times* is aimed at people with more education than most *Sun* readers.

- **Gender:** some writing is aimed more at either men or women.

- **Situation:** a holiday-maker picking up the in-flight magazine will expect easy reading. The same person might make more effort in reading a computer manual.

3 The main *purposes* in writing are to:

- **imagine**, **explore** or **entertain**

- **inform**, **explain** or **describe**

- **persuade**, **argue** or **advise**.

4 Within the main types of *purpose* listed in 3, there are many more exact ones:

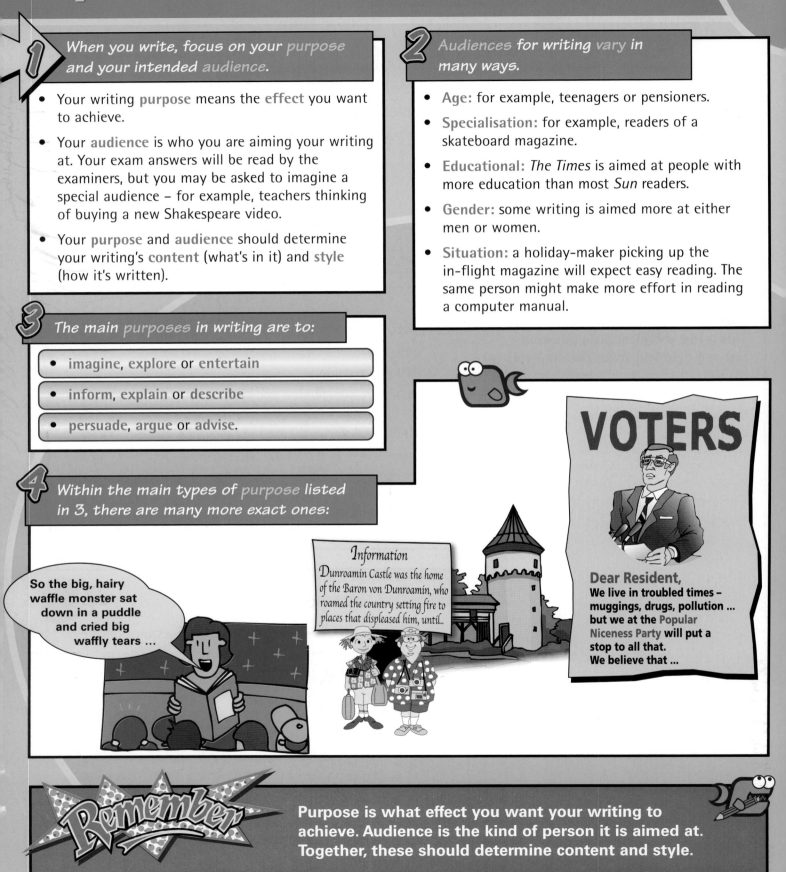

So the big, hairy waffle monster sat down in a puddle and cried big waffly tears …

Information
Dunroamin Castle was the home of the Baron von Dunroamin, who roamed the country setting fire to places that displeased him, until..

VOTERS

Dear Resident,
We live in troubled times – muggings, drugs, pollution … but we at the Popular Niceness Party will put a stop to all that.
We believe that …

Remember

Purpose is what effect you want your writing to achieve. Audience is the kind of person it is aimed at. Together, these should determine content and style.

Work-out!

Copy and complete

purpose

imagine _____
inform _____
persuade _____

+

content

2 mins

1 What is the purpose of:
a a TV advert?
b an election leaflet?
c a humorous novel?
2 How would the audience for 'Biker's Weekly' differ from that of the 'Daily Mail'?
3 What are style and content?

Question and model answer

Write a short article expressing your views on whether or not foreign holidays are a good thing, to be published in a holiday magazine.

More and more people nowadays go on foreign holidays. This may seem innocent enough [1]. After all, many people believe that travel broadens the mind and that getting out of our normal environment helps us to leave our worries behind. Others argue that foreign travel helps us to understand people in other countries, and that this encourages international goodwill and world peace [2].

Although there is something in these arguments, there is much to be said against foreign holidays [3]. First, air travel uses a huge amount of resources, both in aircraft manufacture and fuel. This in turn causes pollution. Then there is the need for airports, which destroy wildlife habitats, as well as being a noise nuisance for local people [4]. Second, tourism may destroy the character and way of life of the countries visited. Lastly, the tourist runs the risk of tropical diseases, snakebites, and even terrorism, quite apart from the expense of the holiday [5].

In short, though foreign holidays may offer some benefits, these are outweighed by the cost to the environment, local economies and the tourist's well-being [6].

Comments

1 Establishes the context and hints at possible problems.

2 Writer makes an impression of fairness by giving arguments in favour.

3 Acknowledges arguments in favour and signals that arguments against are about to come.

4 Varies sentence length and uses sub-clauses effectively.

5 Systematically argues against on three grounds, clearly signposting ('First …').

6 Sums up, stating a clear conclusion.

Now try this!

Write a letter to the magazine arguing in favour of foreign holidays.

Word choice: vocabulary and meaning

1 **If you have a good vocabulary, you'll know what the word means.**

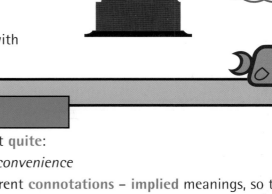

This is a cat-as-trophe!

- Your **vocabulary** is the range of words whose meaning you know and which you can confidently use in your writing.
- The **bigger** your vocabulary, the more **choice** you'll have.
- **Improve** your vocabulary by **reading**. Look up words you don't understand.
- Help your **memory** by writing new words in a **notebook**, with their meanings. Or make up a visual **memory aid**.

2 **The meaning of 'meaning' may seem obvious, but ...**

- Many English words mean **almost** the same thing, but not **quite**:

  happy / contented   sad / miserable   nuisance / inconvenience

- Even words with the same **literal** meaning can have different **connotations** – **implied** meanings, so that they hint at different things. *Danger* and *menace* mean the same, but *menace* hints at something slightly evil, not just risky.

- This can even change slightly according to the sentence in which they appear:

You're a complete menace!

He's got an air of menace about him.

3 **You also need to vary your word choice to achieve variety and avoid repetition:**

- *The fire burned all night, a raging fire, a huge fire visible for miles.*   ✗

- *The fire burned all night, a raging furnace, a huge conflagration visible for miles.*   ✓

Remember

Increase your vocabulary by reading and using a dictionary. Choose words for meaning and connotation, and for variety.

Copy and complete

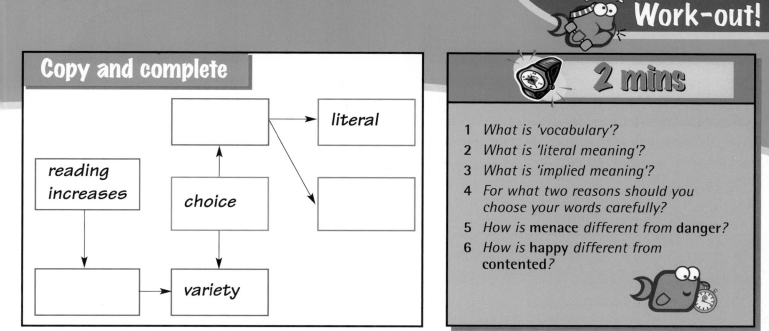

reading increases

choice

literal

variety

1 What is 'vocabulary'?
2 What is 'literal meaning'?
3 What is 'implied meaning'?
4 For what two reasons should you choose your words carefully?
5 How is **menace** different from **danger**?
6 How is **happy** different from **contented**?

Question and model answer

Fill in the gaps in the following passage, choosing the most appropriate word or phrase from the ones given.

One time, however, we were near [fighting/ quarrelling/ having a barney]. He said the [nicest/ pleasantest/ best] manner of spending a hot July day was lying from morning till evening on a bank of heath in the middle of the moors, with the bees [humming/ buzzing/ droning] dreamily about among the bloom, and the larks singing high up over head, and the blue sky and [blinding/ dazzling/ bright] sun shining steadily and cloudlessly.

(Emily Brontë, *Wuthering Heights*)

The most appropriate words are: quarrelling, pleasantest, humming, bright.

Now try this!

Choose appropriate words in the passage below, which continues from the one above.

That was his most [great/ perfect/ brilliant] idea of heaven's happiness: mine was rocking in a rustling green tree, with a west wind blowing, and bright, white clouds flitting [hastily/ rapidly/ fast] above; and not only larks, but throstles, and blackbirds, and linnets, and cuckoos [belting/ pouring/ gushing] out music on every side, and the moors seen at a distance, broken into cool dusky dells; but close by great swells of long grass [undulating/ waving/ bobbing] in waves to the breeze; and woods and sounding water, and the whole world awake and wild with joy.

Comment

'Quarrelling' suggests an argument, while 'fighting' could be physical, and 'having a barney' is too casual in tone. 'Nicest' and 'best' are too vague and general. 'Humming' fits the mood of gentle pleasure and goes with 'dreamily'; 'buzzing' would sound too busy, and is a cliché as applied to bees (it is over-used), and 'droning' sounds boring. Both 'blinding' and 'dazzling' sound uncomfortable, but 'bright' is just right.

Qualifiers

1 Qualifiers (terms of qualification) are words and phrases that provide more information **about** adjectives.

- They enable you to be more **precise** in descriptions.
- They give **variety** to your language and can help to establish **tone**.
- They can **strengthen** a statement.

  slightly balding   *moderately* difficult   *utterly* ruthless

2 Some qualifiers are shown in use below:

3 Many qualifiers simply *add force* to a statement ('That half-pipe is totally awesome ...'), but some can be ranked in order of strength:

> hardly   **slightly**   partly   **fairly**
>
> **extremely**   totally
>
> infinitely   mind-bogglingly

4 Qualifiers can be used rhetorically for *persuasive* effect:

- *It's slightly absurd to spend £30,000 on a banquet in aid of famine relief.* (Understatement)
- *He's astonishingly stupid.* (Exaggeration)

Qualifiers add information about adjectives. They make your writing more precise and varied. They can add force to a statement, or adjust its 'volume'. They can be used in persuasive writing.

Work-out!

Copy and complete

Qualifiers provide _____

about _____ . They can

add _____ to a

statement or be ranked to show

varying degrees of _____ .

2 mins

1 Which of the following are not qualifiers?

> slightly ordinary fully innocently partially
> entirely normally partly marginally

2 Rank these in order of strength:

> extremely fairly hardly infinitely
> mind-bogglingly partly slightly totally

3 What two rhetorical devices can use qualifiers?

Question and model answer

Fill in the gaps using suitable words from the box below.

When I heard the talk I must admit I was .... bored, although the slides were .... interesting. However, my boyfriend Wayne was .... keen to have a go, so – .... reluctantly – I agreed to sign up for it. I go jogging, so I'm .... fit, so I wasn't worried on that score. We had to be weighed to get the bungee length right. I was surprised to find that Wayne weighed only .... more than me – about a kilo. Of course when we did the jump Wayne was .... nervous beforehand. He kept disappearing to the toilet. We jumped from a bridge, and I remember the river rushed towards me .... quickly, but it was .... exciting. I'd recommend it to anyone. It's .... brilliant!

> absolutely utterly wholly infinitely very quite a bit incredibly unbelievably almost
> astonishingly moderately reasonably more or less desperately totally fractionally
> mind-bogglingly breathtakingly pathetically really somewhat pretty

Here are suggested qualifiers from the box, in order:
slightly, quite, really, somewhat, reasonably, fractionally, desperately, astonishingly, breathtakingly, absolutely.

Comment
In some cases, a different word would do as well.

Now try this!

Fill in the gaps below with words from the box above.

I'm .... convinced I saw a ghost that night. I went to turn on the heating as the fire was .... out and I was .... cold. (I tried to do without as my earnings were .... small.) I'm usually .... down to earth, but as I got up, there was an .... loud thunderclap outside. Then a flash of lightning lit the room and I saw a pale figure moving towards me. I was .... petrified!

Making sense: clauses and punctuation

1 A *sentence* makes sense on its own. There are four types:

- **Statement** – the commonest: *Cats eat mice.*
- **Question** – *What do mice eat?*
- **Command** – *Run for your life!*
- **Exclamation** – *Rubbish!*

2 *Most sentences (except exclamations) contain a subject (a noun naming a thing or person) and a verb (a 'doing' word):*

- *The bomb* (subject) *dropped* (verb).
- *Stan* (subject) *ran* (verb).

3 *Many sentences include an object – the thing to which something is done:*

- *The bomb* (subject) *dropped* (verb) *on Stan* (object).
- *The dog* (subject) *ate* (verb) *your dinner* (object).

4 A *compound* sentence links two sentences, using *and*, *but* or *so* (with a comma if a pause seems necessary):

- *I like you, so I don't want to see you get hurt.*
- *Sleep is a mystery but we know we can't do without it.*

5 A *clause* is part of a sentence.

- The **main clause** makes sense on its own:
  Shaun made lasagne ...
- A **sub-clause** adds information, **before**, **after**, or **in the middle** of a main clause, using **connectives** (which, when, where, who):

  Shaun made lasagne, which was all he could cook.

  Not being an expert chef, Shaun made lasagne, which was ...

  Shaun, who was not an expert chef, made lasagne.

6 Using clauses makes your writing more *interesting*, but you must *punctuate* correctly.

- **Begin** a sentence with a **capital** and end it with a **full stop**:

I was bored, I went to the park, my friends were there	✗
I was bored. I went to the park. My friends were there.	✓

- It is often better to turn **short sentences** into a **single longer one** using **commas** to separate clauses:

  Being bored, I went to the park, where I found my friends.

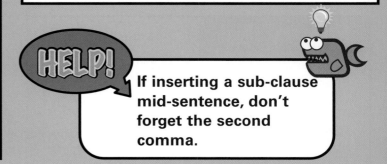

Remember

Sentences make sense. They begin with a capital and end with a full stop. Most contain a subject and verb; many contain an object. A compound sentence joins simple sentences. It is often better to combine short sentences using commas.

HELP!

If inserting a sub-clause mid-sentence, don't forget the second comma.

Work-out!

Copy and complete

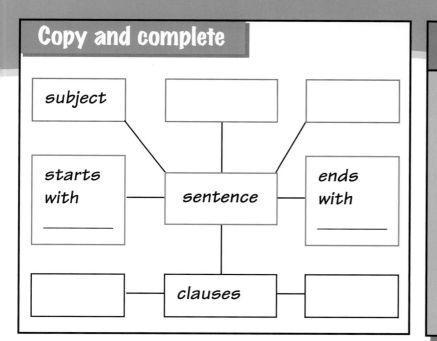

subject

starts with _____

sentence

ends with _____

clauses

2 mins

1 Identify the subject, verb and object in:
   a Duncan rides a bike.
   b Horses love sugar lumps.
   c I don't eat meat.
2 What kind of sentence needs no verb?
3 Turn the following into one sentence with commas:
   My PC is two years old. It has no CD writer.
4 Turn the following into a compound sentence:
   I'm tired. I'm going to sleep.

Question and model answer

Rewrite the following, turning simple sentences into clauses of longer sentences where appropriate. Be careful to use the correct punctuation and connectives.

I got into his car. It was an old Ford Anglia. It was blue. It was sprayed with mud. He drove in silence. He had one hand on the wheel. He had the other on the gun. I decided to wait till traffic lights. Then I would grab the wheel. I would do it while we were still moving slowly. I would force the car off the road.

I got into his car, which was an old Ford Anglia, blue but sprayed with mud. He drove in silence, with one hand on the wheel and the other on the gun. I decided to wait till traffic lights, then, while we were still moving slowly, grab the wheel and force the car off the road.

Comment
This rewrite produces a less jerky paragraph, using the correct punctuation, changing word order and adding connectives where necessary.

Now try this!

Rewrite the following, adapting simple sentences in the same way.

She wore an overcoat. It had once been pink. It was now uniformly grey. On her head was a beret. It had been donated by a schoolgirl. The girl had taken pity on her. Her possessions were bundled into a supermarket trolley. They didn't amount to much. They were soaking wet.

Colons, semicolons and dashes

1 Colons, semicolons and dashes are punctuation marks that you could do without but:

- They can make your writing more precise and more interesting.
- They will help you get a level 7 if you use them well.

2 A colon (:) prepares the reader for information (especially a list) or shows reasoning:

- *Here's what I think: you got scared and hid the body.*
- *Stardom requires several qualities: determination, a big ego, and a little talent.*
- *He wasn't about to give up: he'd come all the way from Texas.*

3 A semicolon (;) is similar to a comma but stronger; it can be used:

- with a colon in a list, especially where items within the list require commas:

  We took all we needed: tents, with sleeping bags; food, water and whisky; and several stuffed badgers.

- where a comma seems too weak, and a full stop too strong:

  A dog barked; a few chickens scattered; a door swung on its hinges.

- between two balanced or contrasting statements:

  They were different. Lara was fiery and impatient; Brad was a steady plodder.

4 Dashes (−) can sometimes be used in place of commas or colons.

- They give a sense of **breaking off** and create an **informal**, **energetic** tone:

  My gerbil – the only friend I had – was about to become toast.

  There's one problem with this place – you!

  'But I'm –' he spluttered.

HELP!

If inserting information before a sub-clause, no second dash is needed: the comma is enough. Example:

Dave hated mustard – even his mother's, which was a pity because …

Remember

A colon prepares the reader for information; a semicolon is slightly stronger than a comma and can be used in lists with commas and between balanced statements; dashes give a sense of breaking off.

Copy and complete

:	colon	prepares reader for _____
;		stronger than a _____
—		gives a sense of _____

Question and model answer

Write a paragraph demonstrating the use of colons, semicolons and dashes.

Big cats – not overgrown toms, but panthers and similarly non-domestic felines – are reported in Britain fairly often. This is surprising: Britain is not noted for its jungle habitats. Nonetheless, sightings have been claimed in widely scattered areas: on Bodmin Moor, Dartmoor, Exmoor and in the relatively tame Wye Valley. The people are not usually mad, although they vary in response: some are delighted; others are terrified. There have been other indications too: scats – big-cat droppings; mutilated sheep left hanging, as if by leopards, in trees; and some fairly persuasive paw prints. The evidence – unless it is the work of hoaxers – speaks for itself.

2 mins

1 Add colons to:
  a Here's my theory the butler did it.
  b Three reasons it's cold, it's wet and I'm tired.
2 Add colons and semicolons to:
  a To make mistakes is human to forgive them is divine.
  b Facilities include squash courts a pool, sauna and jacuzzi and a fitness suite.
3 Add dashes to:
  a The intruder if there had ever been one was gone.
  b Get out of here scram!

Comment

The paragraph uses all three punctuation marks in almost all possible ways. Only the dash for interrupted speech is omitted. The punctuation helps to vary the style. In particular, the dash adds a sense of immediacy – as if the writer is sharing his or her thoughts.

Now try this!

Add colons, semicolons and dashes to the following where indicated by [?].

An 11-year-old boy had a narrow escape [?] in a field [?] not far from his home [?] he spotted what he thought was his pet cat in long grass. Going to stroke it, he soon found his head in the jaws of a black panther. An expert later explained [?] it was playing with the boy. Another expert advised anyone encountering a big cat [?] don't scream or run [?] this could provoke an attack [?] keep still [?] remain standing to assert dominance [?] let the animal wander off.

Passive sentences, tenses, ambiguity

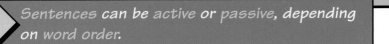

1 Sentences **can be** active or passive, depending **on** word order.

- **Active:** *The butler stole the silver tray.* (subject, active verb, object)
- **Passive:** *The silver tray was stolen by the butler.* (object, passive verb, subject)
- **Active sentences** are clear-cut and keep up the pace. If in doubt, use them.
- **Passive sentences** can be useful for variety and to emphasise the **object** in a sentence:
  The silver tray was stolen by the butler, but the vase is a mystery.
- A passive sentence is often more **formal** and **impersonal** – useful for avoiding responsibility:
  Looters will be shot (not *We will shoot looters*).

2 Tenses **relate to** time, and must be used consistently, **not mixed up:**

Past	Present	Future	Conditional
He looked for it.	*Bilbo finds the ring.*	*We will get home.*	*If you were to ask, I'd go.*
Past perfect	**Present perfect**	**Future perfect**	**Past conditional**
He had lost hope.	*He has escaped.*	*We will have tried.*	*If I'd known, I'd have gone.*

3 **Ambiguity** means having two or more possible meanings:

- *Joe gave Winston his sandwich.* (Whose sandwich?)
- *My cousin is a disturbed dog trainer.* (Who's disturbed?)
- *How did you find the soup?* (By looking in the bowl?)
- *Go and feed the lions with Eric.* (Feed Eric to the lions?)
- *She drowned after lunch in the bath.*
  (She ate lunch in the bath?)

4 **Ambiguity,** if unintended, can be avoided by rewording or by punctuation:

- *Go with Eric and feed the lions.*
- *She drowned after lunch, in the bath.*
  (unless she ate lunch in the bath!)

HELP!

Use the present tense to give the plot of a novel, play or film (*Bilbo sees a troll …*).

Remember

Passive sentences emphasise the object.

Tenses must be used consistently.

Avoid unintended double meanings by rewording or punctuation.

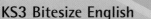

Copy and complete

1 active
2

sentences

Avoid ambiguity by:
1
2

Main tenses:
1 past
2
3
4

1 Change active to passive:
   a A lion ate Eric.
   b A bus ran over my lunch box.
2 Change passive to active:
   a She is ignored by everyone.
   b I was stung by a bee.
3 What tense should you use to describe a plot?
4 Which word causes confusion? My father came with my uncle and offered me his hand.

Question and model answer

In the following paragraph:
1 **Change the two most appropriate sentences from active to passive.**
2 **Make the tenses consistent.**
3 **Make ambiguous sentences clear.**

In 'Zombies for Ever', zombies kill a man walking home at night. After that, he became a zombie himself and prowls around looking for his wife. He finds her and her love brings him back to life. Unfortunately a mob accuse him of murdering his brothers and lynch him. His wife forgave them.

Present tense for plot

In 'Zombies for Ever', a man walking home at night is killed by zombies. After that, he becomes a zombie himself and prowls around looking for his wife. He finds her and her love brings him back to life. Unfortunately he is accused of murdering his brothers by a mob and lynched. His wife forgives the mob.

Passive emphasises man as victim and avoids ambiguity

Present for plot; repeat 'mob' to make it clear who is forgiven

Now try this!

Do the same with the following – but only change one sentence to passive, and correct the conditional at the end.

William landed near modern-day Hastings. The Norman knights charged the Saxons on horseback but the Saxons fight bravely and almost win. Things went downhill for them after an arrow hit Harold in the eye. If it hadn't been for this, English history might turn out very differently.

Formal and informal English

1 It is important to write with an appropriate degree of *formality*.

- **Formal** language need not be **long-winded** or 'posh'.

- It **must** be in **standard English** – the kind spoken by newsreaders – so that all English speakers can understand.

- It must **avoid slang** and **phrases** that sound **too casual**.

2 This newspaper hasn't got standard English right:

Evening Non-Standard

The Boss, right, is getting pretty steamed up about schoolkids bunking off to hang with their homeys and play one armed bandits.

He says if parents don't get it together and sort it pronto, they is going to be coughing up the readies or getting banged up for a bit – innit.

3 *Non-standard English* is used in *dialect* (*local speech*) or by particular *social groups* (*e.g. skateboarders*).

- **It can't** be used in an **essay**, but is acceptable in **dialogue** (speech in a story or play).

- It differs from **standard English** in several ways:

Grammar (sentence structure)

> So he goes, 'Give it to I!'

Vocabulary (individual words)

> I did the ollie but I bailed on the shoveit!

Idioms (expressions with a special meaning)

> He was one prawn short of a seafood salad – if you know what I mean.

4 *Contractions* (*words that run together using an apostrophe*) *make writing less formal.*

- **Examples:** *I'll* (I will); *Don't* (Do not); *You'll* (You will).

- **Don't overuse** them in an essay.

- **Use them** in **dialogue** to make it seem more natural.

Remember

Write with an appropriate degree of formality. Use standard English (no dialect, slang or very casual phrases) in an essay. You can use non-standard English in dialogue.

Copy and complete

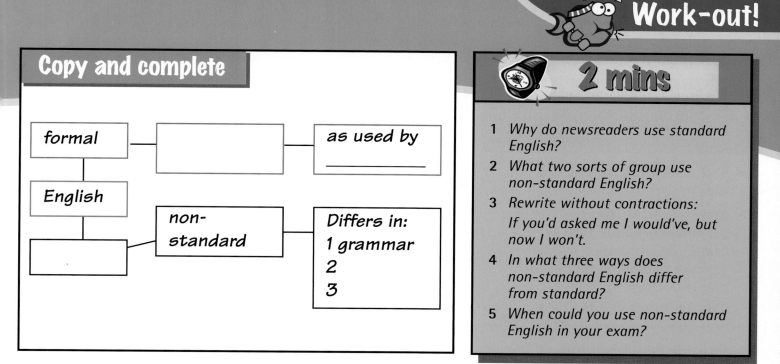

formal — [___] — as used by _____

English

[___] — non-standard — Differs in:
1 grammar
2
3

1 Why do newsreaders use standard English?
2 What two sorts of group use non-standard English?
3 Rewrite without contractions: If you'd asked me I would've, but now I won't.
4 In what three ways does non-standard English differ from standard?
5 When could you use non-standard English in your exam?

Question and model answer

1 Rewrite the newspaper article opposite in formal standard English.
2 Explain why this is appropriate.

1 The Prime Minister is very concerned about schoolchildren truanting to spend time with their friends and play fruit machines. He says that if parents fail to get this behaviour under control quickly they will have to pay fines or face prison sentences.

2 A newspaper needs to use standard English in order to be understood by as many people as possible. Standard English also sounds more responsible, especially when reporting on a serious issue.

Comments

1 The rewritten version replaces non-standard vocabulary, such as 'Boss' for Prime Minister and 'homeys' for friends. It rephrases idioms such as 'hang with' for 'spend time with'. Non-standard grammar – the insertion of 'right', 'they is' and 'innit' (isn't it) at the end – has been eliminated.

2 Correctly identifies two reasons:
a) to be understood
b) to create the right impression.

Now try this!

Rewrite the following in formal, standard English:

I was, like, just chillin' when I hears a big rumpus outside. I runs out onto the street and sees this geezer laying into this kid. I says to him, 'Lay off the kid!' He says, 'You 'avin a laugh or what?' Then a copper comes and he legs it.

Paragraphing

1 Paragraphs **split text into manageable sections and show the development of ideas.**

- There should generally be **one major idea** in each paragraph.
- Make paragraphs **shorter** if writing for **children**, for the **Web**, or for a **leaflet**. (In these cases you can't rely as much as usual on your reader's concentration.)

2 Ordering **your paragraphs depends on subject matter.**

- If using a system such as **Mind Mapping** or **spidergrams** to plan and structure an essay, it may be that each branch of your diagram can become a paragraph.
- **Opening** and **closing** paragraphs are especially important – for getting your reader's attention and pulling ideas together.
- One way to **order** paragraphs is **chronologically** – in order of events. This is the obvious way to order a story, a historical account or a crime report.
- **Another way** is in order of **importance**. You might choose to deal with the most important things **first**, or – if you're arguing a case – to save them **till the end**.

1 Introduction: Whales are great!	2 The threat	3 Why save whales?	4 What we can do
There can be few sights more awesome than …	Yet, sadly, these beautiful creatures …	If this threat just affected the whales themselves, that would be bad enough. However, …	Despite this, there is still time to take action …

3 Structure within paragraphs is **also important.**

- It helps if each paragraph **begins** with some indication of its **main idea**.
- After the first paragraph, it also helps the reader if you show how the paragraph **relates to the previous one**. Do this using a **link word** or **phrase** (see 'Structure', page 28).
- The **middle** of the paragraph should develop this.
- The **end** may give a sense of **closure** or hint at what is to come:

  … but we were wrong, as we soon found out.

Remember

Paragraphs make text manageable. Order them carefully. Try to include a main idea in each one. Aim for development within each paragraph too. Use beginnings to tell the reader what to expect.

Copy and complete

Paragraphs make text _____ . Their
_____ shows the development of your
ideas. You can signal what is to come
by using _____ words and phrases.
Structure within the paragraph is
important too. The _____ should
suggest what the paragraph is about.

2 mins

1   What should your first paragraph do?
2   What should your last paragraph do?
3   Which of these is not a link word?

> however moreover often
> nevertheless yet

4   Name two ways to order paragraphs.

Question and model answer

Put the following paragraphs in order
and explain what the main idea is in
each one.

A However, many researchers are
concerned. Some say TV has turned
us into passive consumers who just
watch the world without being involved
in it. Others say that people were
happier when they entertained
themselves, and that TV stunts
children's imagination.

B Despite its slow beginnings, TV is now
the number one pastime of the West.
Many people watch several hours of it
every day. If offers relaxation, cultural
enrichment and information, and
keeps us abreast of important
events.

C Whatever the pros and cons, TV is
unlikely to go out of fashion for many
years to come. However, new
technology such as digital TV may at
least make us more interactive and
less passive in our viewing. We can
only hope so.

D Television was invented by John Logie
Baird in 1926, yet few homes had a
set until the mid 1950s. At first, all
TV was black and white, colour being
invented in the 1950s and finding its
way into British homes in the 1960s
and 1970s.

The order is D, B, A, C.

Comment

Paragraph D introduces the subject, going back to
TV's early history. Paragraph B begins with a link
word ('Despite') referring back to this. This
paragraph gives the advantages of TV. The link word
'However' at the start of paragraph A signals that
it will at least partly contradict what has gone
before – which it does, by voicing researchers' fears.
The conclusion (paragraph C) is signalled by the link
phrase 'Whatever the pros and cons', referring back
to paragraphs B and A. It looks to the future,
hoping that developments will overcome the
possible disadvantages given in paragraph A.

Now try this!

Expand the ideas
and paragraph
openings given
opposite into a
short essay on
saving the whale.
Focus on one main
idea in each
paragraph, and
structure each
paragraph well.

Structuring a story

- It is worth spending time **planning** this – even in an exam! Good planning will **improve** the story and make it **easier** to write.

2 There are many ways to structure a story.

- One good way is:
  opening, development, complication, crisis, resolution (ODCCR).

Opening

Catch the reader's attention. You could begin with action, a quirky character detail, or an arresting line of dialogue. Make readers want to know more.

Do I have to?

Development

This builds up the plot from its starting point and involves the reader. We could see the seeds of a problem growing.

Complication

A story in which everything goes smoothly and predictably is dull. A complication creates tension. Readers want to know how it will be resolved.

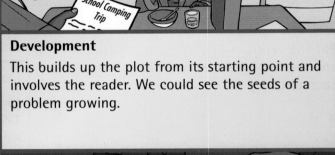

Don't say where we've gone.

The tide – we're cut off!

Crisis

The dramatic climax. At this point, readers should be 'on the edge of their seats' wondering what will happen next.

Resolution

How the story is wound up. It may end happily (e.g. hero kills villain and marries heroine), but not always. The tension must be ended, questions answered, so that readers have a sense of completion.

Remember

Structure your story. Get the reader's attention, show development and a complication. Stage a crisis and show how it is resolved.

PLEASE DO NOT WRITE
IN THIS BOOK-
Use your own paper to work
through the questions.
THANK YOU

Copy and complete

opening	gets reader's attention
	builds up plot
complication	
	dramatic climax
resolution	

2 mins

1 Give three ways in which you might catch the reader's attention.
2 Which stage of the structure involves the reader?
3 Why does there need to be a complication?
4 What should the reader be wondering at the crisis point?
5 What must the reader feel for there to be a resolution?

Question and model answer

Write the start of a story about going on a school camp.

The letter lay crumpled up at the bottom of my school bag. I'd thought about not showing it to Mum. But then I thought she'd be bound to find out somehow. She likes to 'swap notes' with other mums on just about everything. I'm the opposite. I don't know why, but when I go to tell Mandy or Lakshmi or someone what I did at the weekend, it sounds stupid and comes out wrong. So half the time I don't bother.

I wheeled in my bike – handed down from my brother Kevin, and propped it against the wall. Mum was in the kitchen.

'Hallo, Suzi,' she said brightly. 'How was school?'

'I've got a letter,' I answered. Her face clouded. She probably thought I was in trouble. In a way I was.

'Here,' I said, pulling the letter out from under some dog-eared exercise books and plonking it down on the table.

She opened it. 'Oh – school camp at Burpham-on-Sea!' she said with relief.

'Yeah,' I answered. 'Do I have to go?'

Comment

This engages our interest. The letter mystery arouses our curiosity. We wonder what it is and why Suzi doesn't want her mother to read it. We also find out about Suzi and her family. She has friends but is not close to them. She is not very confident, and doesn't want to go on camp. The fact that she rides her brother's old bike implies that the family is not well off. The dog-eared exercise books imply that Suzi is not keen on school. It is also implied that she has been in trouble before, and that the camp may bring more trouble.

Now try this!

Write the resolution section to the story shown opposite. You could begin: 'The tide – we're cut off!' Make it Suzi's story if you wish.

Telling the story: narrative devices

1 When you tell a story, you choose your narrative devices:

- **Narrative viewpoint** – the point of view from which you tell the story.

- **Reveal or withhold information** – the reader is in your hands.

- **Tense** – you will probably use past tense, but you could use present.

- **Pace** – you can vary it, both by **what happens** and by your **focus**. For example, you might focus very **closely** on someone defusing a bomb, describing it in **detail**.

2 Character can be revealed in several ways:

- **Commentary**: *Dana was a happy-go-lucky girl who thought that ...*

- **What characters do**: *Iqbal left the other toffee for his grandmother.*

- **What they say** (in dialogue): *'I don't take kindly to being made a fool of!'*

- **First person narrative** ('I ... me ... my' – see page 20) reveals the narrator's character by how he or she tells the story.

3 Now see some narrative devices in action:

Present tense – immediacy, close focus

Aaron gets the sharp end of the bar in between the manhole and the cobbles. He has very little time. Already he hears dogs barking, cries in Yiddish, orders spoken sharply in German. Working the tip into the crack, he levers up the cover by a centimetre, two centimetres, gets his fingers on the lip, and pulls. He barely notices a face at a window watching as the cover heaves up, or the reek as it does. Later, too late, he will recall that face.

Viewpoint shifts, author comments

He slides the cover aside, fearfully slots himself into the gap, clinging to a rusting ladder with one hand and scraping the cover back into place with the other. Darkness. Pounding – his heart. The dogs are close now. Marching boots. German voices above him. His grandmother used to say, 'In the darkness, hope.' He lets go of the rung, and falls.

Flashback

Suspense – will he succeed?

Flash forward; information witheld (Who? Why 'too late'?)

Impressions, sounds

Remember

You are in charge of how your story is told. You choose the viewpoint, how you reveal and withhold information, the tense, the pace and focus, and how to show character.

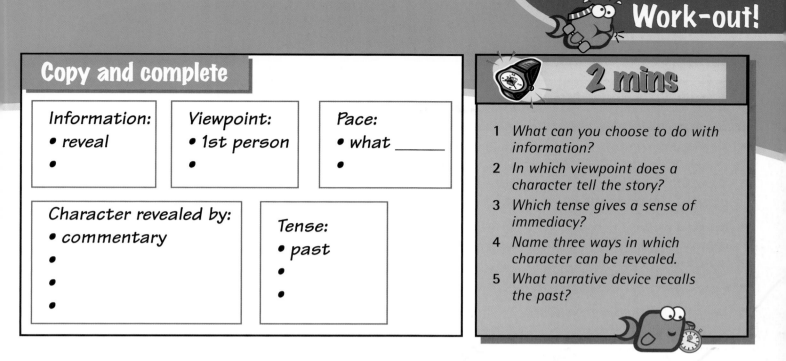

Copy and complete

Information:
• reveal
•

Viewpoint:
• 1st person
•

Pace:
• what _____
•

Character revealed by:
• commentary
•
•
•

Tense:
• past
•
•

2 mins

1 What can you choose to do with information?
2 In which viewpoint does a character tell the story?
3 Which tense gives a sense of immediacy?
4 Name three ways in which character can be revealed.
5 What narrative device recalls the past?

Question and model answer

Continue the story begun opposite in the past tense, conveying Aaron's experience as vividly as possible.

When he regained consciousness, it was with a jolt. For a moment he had no idea where he was. Then it came to him – he was in a Berlin sewer. The smell dispelled any doubts. His body hurt all over; he was cold and wet. Looking up, he could make out a glimmer of light, perhaps five metres away. But there were no sounds coming from above, only from around him in the darkness: trickling water, and a thin squeaking that seemed to move away from him.

He reached into his pocket, and with relief found matches and lit one, revealing in its yellow halo a stooping-height circular brick tunnel running with slimy water. He looked at his watch. It had shattered in the fall and was stopped at half-past two. How long had he been unconscious? He had no idea.

Comment

This is a level 7 answer because it conveys Aaron's experience so well. The narrative viewpoint is third person, but we identify with Aaron, seeing through his eyes. Therefore any information about his fall, or how long he has been unconscious, is withheld. We experience through his senses: the smell, the sounds – including the meaning implied in the 'thin squeaking', his aches, the 'yellow halo of light'. We note his relief and his loss of any sense of time, the question at the end reflecting his thoughts.

Now try this!

Continue the story up to the point where Aaron emerges from the sewer. Try to use some of the narrative devices you have learned so far.

Commentary, description and dialogue

1 Commentary **refers to** direct insight **into character and events given by an author.**

- **Nineteenth-century** writers often addressed the reader:

  You might imagine, dear reader, that Fanny was at a loss. However, she hated to admit defeat.

- **Modern** writers rarely use the 'Dear reader' approach, and often let us **draw our own conclusions** about characters.

- **As a writer**, you can **comment** on characters:

  Donna was afraid and confused.

- But it can be more effective to let readers interpret the evidence:

  Donna trembled. 'I – I'll stay. No – I'll come with you,' she said, uncertainly.

2 Description **means** telling **readers about something.**

- **Action**:

  She reached slowly for the blue wire, and cut it.

  The detonator continued to tick. She wiped the sweat from her forehead.

- **Appearance**:

  Jane was smooth-featured, with coffee-cream skin and deep brown eyes. Her mouth was full-lipped and smiling.

- **Setting**:

  The first rays of the spring sun played on the water below Kew Bridge.

  There were gulls moving methodically across a glistening mudbank far below.

3 Description **helps readers to** imagine **themselves in the story, but:**

- **Too much** of it – especially of **appearance** and **setting** – can slow the **pace** too much. It is often better to **hint**, using key details to get the reader's imagination working:

  Piers had the kind of square jaw and steady gaze that inspire confidence.

4 Dialogue **lets** characters **speak for themselves, and can be used to** tell the story.

- It needs to be fairly **realistic**. 'Listen' to it in your head. Can you imagine the characters saying it? But it should always **serve a purpose**.

- **Punctuate** it correctly: **speech marks** for the **actual words spoken** (not for reported speech). Question and exclamation marks go *inside* the closing speech mark. New paragraph for each new speaker.

  Jane sighed. 'We may as well give up.'

  'Don't be ridiculous!' snapped Paul.

Remember

You can comment on characters and events, or let the evidence speak for itself. Description helps readers to imagine. You can also reveal character and tell a story through dialogue.

Copy and complete

commentary v. drawing own _____

description	1 action
	2
	3

dialogue	1 reveals character
	2

2 mins

1 What is the alternative to commentary?
2 What is the risk of using too much description?
3 What should dialogue always have?
4 Put speech marks where needed in:
   a We're lost she said. He told her not to worry.
   b How can we survive? I asked.

Question and model answer

Write the start of a story called 'One more day' using commentary, description and dialogue.

She brushed her little brother's hair, gave him his packed lunch, and pushed him out of the door. 'Be good,' she said. 'Don't dawdle or you'll be late.'

'Sima!' her father shouted downstairs.

'OK, Dad. I'm coming,' she yelled back. She sighed. He had been bedridden for a year now, since the accident. She was a patient girl, energetic and good-natured, but it had become too much. She couldn't stand it anymore.

As she carried her father's breakfast upstairs, she took in the stained carpet, its floral pattern barely visible, the cat claw marks on the banister, the bare light bulb over the landing. 'Just one more day,' she said to herself. 'One more day.'

Comment

This is a level 7 answer because it uses all three narrative types as required, and uses them in an interesting way to tell the story. The description of the stairway conveys the depressing atmosphere of the house. The dialogue (correctly punctuated) suggests Sima's character, which is made clearer by commentary in the sentence beginning 'She was ...'.

Now try this!

Either continue the story for one or two paragraphs, making sure to use commentary, description and dialogue, or write an opening of your own for a story called 'One more day'. Make the subject different, but use the basic framework of commentary, description and dialogue.

Inform, explain, describe

1 This type of writing involves *giving information* to the reader.

- Put yourself 'in the reader's shoes' – **empathise**.
- Think of your **audience**. Who are they? What do they know? What do they need to know? (See 'Purpose and audience', page 36.)
- Consider your **purpose** – what this piece of writing is meant to do.
- **Organise** your text to suit your **audience** and **purpose**.
- Select appropriate **details** and **examples**.

2 Selection is important.

- If **explaining** how to mend a puncture on a bike, remember: readers **may know less than you** (for example, the names of special tools). Include relevant details only:

  The inner tube may smell peculiar, and could be black or pink.

  Bubbles will rise from the puncture hole. Mark its location carefully ... ✓

- **Cut repeated** or **irrelevant** information. If short of space, cut what is **least important**.

3 Examples *are often useful:*

- *Recent theatrical productions have included 'Oklahoma', 'Oliver' and 'Twelfth Night'.*

- *Restaurants are many and varied – Chinese, Bangladeshi, Thai and French, to name a few.*

- *Cities such as Bristol, Manchester and Birmingham have their own airports.*

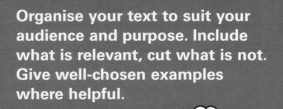

Organise your text to suit your audience and purpose. Include what is relevant, cut what is not. Give well-chosen examples where helpful.

4 Some *types of* information writing:

What to see, where to eat, where to stay.

History, rules, hours.

Tells parents and new students what to expect.

How to do it.

Work-out!

Copy and complete

purpose		for example,
		_____

audience →

| 1 who?
2 what _____ ?
3 what _____ ? | | 1 selection
2 |

2 mins

1 What does empathising with the reader mean?
2 What two things must you select in informative writing?
3 What two things should you cut out?
4 What should you then cut if short of space?
5 When might you use the phrase 'to name a few'?

Question and model answer

Write the text of an introductory talk to prepare 14-year-olds practically for a sport they are about to try for the first time.

Signals what's coming →

There are several things you need to know about caving. First, what to bring with you. We supply lights and helmets but not clothes. Wear old clothes as they could get damaged, and they're bound to get muddy. You also need a change of clothes and a towel, as you may get wet. As to footwear, anything strong and with a good grip will do, such as wellies. But again, don't wear your best trainers. It's also a good idea to bring a snack and a drink for afterwards.

← **Gives reasons**

← **Information in order of importance**

Signals second part →

Second, how to behave in the cave. Stick together and help each other out when necessary. Listen to my instructions and pass them to the person behind you. Remember to look up from time to time to avoid banging your head. Don't touch any formations. And don't fall behind or the flesh-eating zombies will get you.

← **Clear dos and don'ts**

← **Humour signals end and lightens tone**

Now try this!

Write the contents list and one paragraph for a brochure for your school, intended for new students. Your one paragraph could be the introduction, or it could be on the aspect of the school that most appeals to you. For example, its excellent dinners or sports facilities.

Persuade, argue, advise

1 Writing to *persuade* or *argue* requires a special approach.

- First, **brainstorm** arguments **for** and **against**. This may change your views. If not, it will at least prepare you for **counter-arguments** (arguments against your own).

- Work out a **logical order** in which to present your case. (Numbering will help.)

- You may find it is most effective to **save your best argument** till last.

- Where possible, supply **evidence**. For example, statistics.

- **Quotations**, while not **proving** your case, will add support to it.

PRIVATE KEEP OUT

Property is theft
(Proudhon, 1840)

2 *Signposting – using link words and phrases to guide your reader (see also 'Structure', page 28) – is especially important in persuasive writing.*

- **Phrases** such as *however, nonetheless, despite, on the other hand* are useful.

- For **counter-arguments**, phrases such as *although, in reality, the facts are, quite the opposite is in fact the case* are useful.

- Phrases **giving emphasis** are also useful (either adjectives, or adverbs, ending in *-ly*):

ludicrous   appalling   remarkable

astonishing   incredible   important

huge   above all   absolute

vital   essential

3 *Selling* is a special kind of persuasion.

- Consider why your **target audience** should be interested.

- Emphasise the **reasons for buying** your product.

- Consider (and possibly end with) the **risks** if they don't buy it.

Buy KingCool

Super-tungsten trucks for max flexibility, durability and manoeuvrability.

Or end up like Dwayne.

4 *Advising* is often similar to *persuading.*

- However, it can be more **open-ended**. You may want to help readers **decide**, so phrases like *could, should, might, perhaps* and *on the other hand* will be useful.

Remember

Brainstorm your arguments or selling points, sort them into the most logical or most compelling order, and signpost readers so that they can follow your thinking.

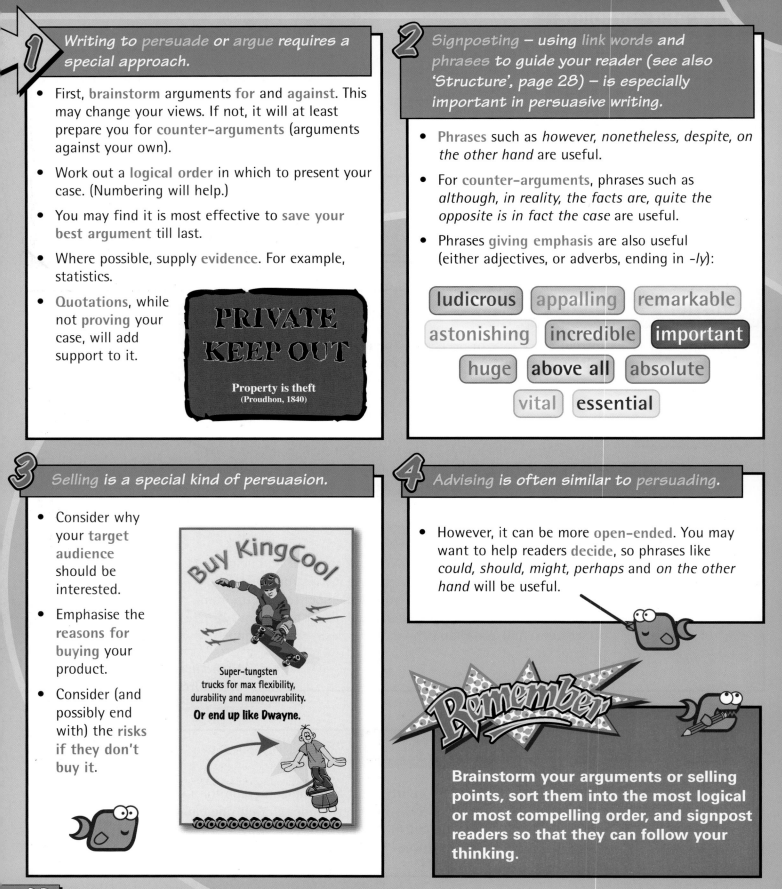

Copy and complete

brainstorm → o_____

e_____ ← q_____

1 *Why bother to think of arguments* **against** *your own?*
2 *Give an example of evidence you might use.*
3 *Which link word or phrase signposts a partial agreement with a point just mentioned?*
   moreover   in addition   however   in fact   certainly
4 *Which word does not give emphasis?*
   ludicrous   nice   appalling   remarkable
5 *When would these words be useful?*
   could   should   might   perhaps

Question and model answer

Write the text of a leaflet to persuade parents to send their children to your school.

Looking for a secondary school for your child? St Ethel's Comprehensive is able to offer all the benefits that concerned parents seek in a school – and more.

It has an excellent academic record, with 70 % of students achieving five or more GCSEs at C-grade or above, and 60 % entering the sixth form. It also offers a wide subject choice, including Urdu at GCSE and Theatre Studies at A/S and A2 level.

However, we at St Ethel's believe that school is not just about passing exams. We pride ourselves on a tutor group system that looks after every student. Moreover, our dedicated staff enthusiastically support a range of after-school activities, including parachuting and photography.

Added to this, we are situated amidst the breathtaking beauty of the Dee Valley, yet easily accessible by bus and train.

We feel sure that St Ethel's will bring out the best in your child. Phone us now ...

Annotations:

- Confidently addresses parents, flatters them – 'concerned'
- Signposts qualifying point
- Positive emotive word choice
- Bonus point signposted; superlative adjective
- Dash used well
- Positive adjectives: 'excellent', 'wide'; evidence (statistics); examples
- Signposts supporting point
- Examples
- Signpost – 'yet'
- Variety in sentence length and structure

Now try this!

Plan and write a similar leaflet for your school, emphasising its positive features. You could use the main subjects of each paragraph above as a framework for your text.

Analyse, review, comment

1 This kind of writing requires you to give a *balanced view* of a situation, text or issue.

- You first need to consider all the **evidence** and possible points of view.
- If **reviewing a novel, play or film** it helps if you can **compare** it with others that are similar. For example, you might find one spy thriller more exciting than another.
- If commenting on a **situation** or **issue**, you may need to look at several **sources** of information.
- You may give **your own views**, but they should be **distinct** from your balanced analysis. *(Personally, I feel that ...)*

2 Several *phrases* are useful (in red in point 3):

- *Those ... may find ...*
- *could prove ... for some ...*
- *On the other hand ...*
- *you may feel that ...*
- *certainly ... However, ...*
- *may be, could be, perhaps, probably, possibly ...*
- *It seems that ...*

3 As always, be aware of your *audience*.

- You should show awareness of different **needs, tastes and preferences**:

  > *Those seeking excitement may find Cyprus too quiet in the evenings.*

  > *Red Rhino's punchy, bass-heavy sound could prove a little raw for some.*

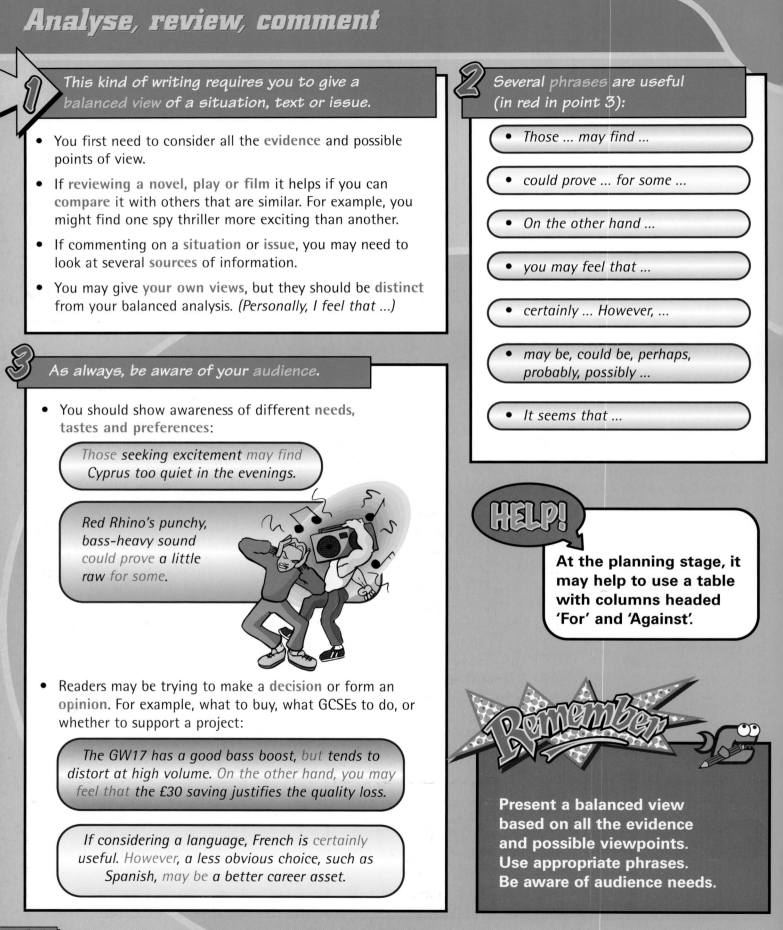

- Readers may be trying to make a **decision** or form an **opinion**. For example, what to buy, what GCSEs to do, or whether to support a project:

  > *The GW17 has a good bass boost, but tends to distort at high volume. On the other hand, you may feel that the £30 saving justifies the quality loss.*

  > *If considering a language, French is certainly useful. However, a less obvious choice, such as Spanish, may be a better career asset.*

HELP!

At the planning stage, it may help to use a table with columns headed 'For' and 'Against'.

Remember

Present a balanced view based on all the evidence and possible viewpoints. Use appropriate phrases. Be aware of audience needs.

Copy and complete

balanced	→	1
_____		2
based on:		

be aware of	→	Phrases, e.g.
_____		1
		2

2 mins

1 Why might someone read a book review?
2 What do you need to weigh up in order to analyse a situation?
3 What do the phrases 'may be, perhaps, probably, possibly' have in common?
4 What word might you use to signpost your own opinion?
5 When would you use the phrase 'on the other hand'?

Question and model answer

Write a review helpfully comparing two novels.

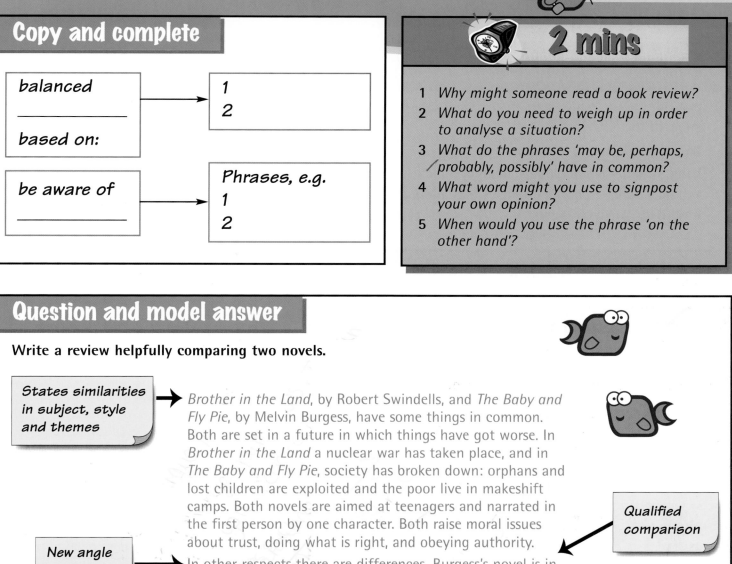

States similarities in subject, style and themes →

Brother in the Land, by Robert Swindells, and *The Baby and Fly Pie*, by Melvin Burgess, have some things in common. Both are set in a future in which things have got worse. In *Brother in the Land* a nuclear war has taken place, and in *The Baby and Fly Pie*, society has broken down: orphans and lost children are exploited and the poor live in makeshift camps. Both novels are aimed at teenagers and narrated in the first person by one character. Both raise moral issues about trust, doing what is right, and obeying authority.

← **Qualified comparison**

New angle signalled →

In other respects there are differences. Burgess's novel is in some ways more pessimistic. No adult can be trusted. It is a 'dog eat dog' world in which trying to 'do the right thing' only leads to brutality. Even the teenage characters are morally unreliable. In the Swindells novel, the situation – post-Holocaust, the planet almost destroyed – is bleaker, yet there is more faith in human goodness. There are ruthless villains, but there are also brave, honest people who care for others.

← **Evidence**

Good final comparison using 'but' →

← **'yet' points to a paradox**

Now try this!

Use the review above as a framework for a review comparing two novels, plays or films. Remember to explain similarities and differences in a balanced way and to signpost your points to your reader.

Spelling: vowel rules

1 English spelling is confusing, but there are several rules relating to vowels (a e i o u).

- Vowels all have a short sound and a long sound (which is also the name of the letter):

  Short: *fat hens rip off nuns*

  Long: *hateful metre strikes hopeful tune*

- You may notice from the examples that **adding an 'e'** to the end of a word (or syllable) changes the short vowel sound to a long one.

Short sound	Long sound
fat	fate
pet	Pete
win	wine
mop	mope
cub	cube

2 A letter 'i' has the same effect (mostly in the present participle of verbs):

- *hating meting lining toting fluting*

- To **prevent** the 'i' from changing the vowel sound from short to long, you have to **double the consonant** before the vowel.

Verb	Present participle	Past participle
tap	tapping	tapped
bet	betting	betted
sin	sinning	sinned
slop	slopping	slopped
gut	gutting	gutted

3 An 'e' ending to a verb makes the vowel sound long.

- When you form a **participle** (adding **–ing** or **–ed**) to a verb ending in 'e', you can drop the 'e' because these endings already change the vowel sound from short to long. Don't double any consonants.

Verb	Present participle	Past participle
tape	taping	taped
invite	inviting	invited
hope	hoping	hoped
slope	sloping	sloped
rule	ruling	ruled

4 Remember: 'i' before 'e' except after 'c' (but only when the sound is 'ee').

- Hence: *belief, relief, brief, chief, thief*; but *ceiling, conceit, deceive, receive*.

- The words *seize* and *weird* are exceptions to the rule.

Remember

Vowels have a short and a long sound. Adding 'e' makes it long. Doubling the consonant before the vowel in an *-ing* or *-ed* word keeps the short vowel sound. And 'i' before 'e' …

Copy and complete

Vowels have a _____ and a _____ sound. Adding 'e' makes it _____ . Doubling the consonant before the _____ in an -ing or -ed word keeps the short _____ sound. And 'i' before _____ .

1 If I'm eating out I'm (dinning/dining).
2 If I'm ahead I'm (winning/wining).
3 If I'm climbing a tree I'm (shinning/shining).
4 How does an 'e' on the end of a word affect its vowel sound?
5 How do you stop verbs that end in 'e' from changing their vowel sound when you add -ing or -ed?
6 Name two exceptions to the 'i before e except after c' rule.

Question and model answer

Correct the mistakes in the paragraph below.

I recieved a letter the other day from an old freind who said he was hopping to see me. My husband was moping the floor at the time and unfortunatly I droped the letter. The next thing I knew it was swiming in the bucket. To my releif, the letter was still readable. The freind was inviteing me to diner. I love to be winned and dinned, but strangly I forgot to go – wierd! Beleive me: next time I get an invitation I'll tap it to the cieling.

I **received** a letter the other day from an old **friend** who said he was **hoping** to see me. My husband was **mopping** the floor at the time and **unfortunately** I **dropped** the letter. The next thing I knew it was **swimming** in the bucket. To my **relief**, the letter was still readable. The **friend** was **inviting** me to **dinner**. I love to be **wined** and **dined**, but **strangely** I forgot to go – **weird**! **Believe** me: next time I get an invitation I'll **tape** it to the **ceiling**.

Comment

You won't get any exam questions on spelling, but in the writing test your spelling will affect your marks. On the other hand, you'll get marks for a good vocabulary, so don't avoid using the perfect word just because you're not quite sure how to spell it. And try to leave time to check your work.

Now try this!

Correct the mistakes.

Darren was takeing his time over his homwork. He was determind not to make any mistaks. He'd recieved a low mark and was hopping to do better. Unfortunatly he'd sloped coffee all over it. He hatted maths. His teacher said he could be a shinning example to the class if he tried, instead of siting in the corner mopping over his misfortuns.

Plurals, verbs and apostrophes

1 For most nouns but not all, making the plural simply requires an 's'.

- If the noun in its singular form ends in 's', 'ch', 'sh' or 'x', add 'es':

  bus/buses hunch/hunches dish/dishes fox/foxes

- If the noun ends in 'y' after a vowel, just add 's' for the plural:

  bays ploys lay-bys rays ways

- If it ends in 'y' after a consonant, replace the 'y' with 'ies':

  rubies babies flies follies lollies

- If it ends in 'o' after a vowel, just add 's'; but if the 'o' is after a consonant, add 'es':

  rodeos radios studios
  but ... *potatoes tomatoes dingoes*

- If it ends in 'f' or 'fe', the plural usually ends in 'ves':

  wives lives loaves leaves sheaves elves
  (**but note:** *chiefs beliefs roofs waifs*)

2 These rules generally apply to the verb forms of these words too:

- *The city buses us to school.*
- *He plays with us.*
- *She flies into a rage.*
- *Dan lives here.*

3 Apostrophes *cause some people a lot of problems!*

- **Never** use one just because a word is plural:

  Some potato's and tomato's for the burrito's. ✗

- **Never** use them for *its* as a pronoun (like his):

  Give the dog it's dinner. ✗

4 Use apostrophes **to show** possession.

- *The potato's skin ... the tomato's colour ... the big girl's blouse*

- **Place** them **after** the 's' if the word is a **plural**:

  The elves' hats ... the twins' room ... the players' shirts

- **But** if the plural **doesn't end in** 's', the apostrophe goes **before** the possessive 's':

  The women's lunches ... the children's faces

- **Collective nouns** such as *team* and *family* are **singular**, so it's *the team's shirts*.

5 Use apostrophes **to show that something has been** left out (omission).

- *I can't* (can not), *he won't* (will not), *they're* (they are) *ill.*

- *She didn't* (did not) *come till six o'clock* (of the clock).

- And in **dialogue** a character might say:
  'Poor 'Arold 'as got an 'orrible 'ernia.'

Plurals of words ending in 's', 'ch', 'sh', 'x', 'y', 'o' and 'f' need special attention. Apostrophes should only ever be used to show possession and omission.

Remember

Work-out!

Copy and complete

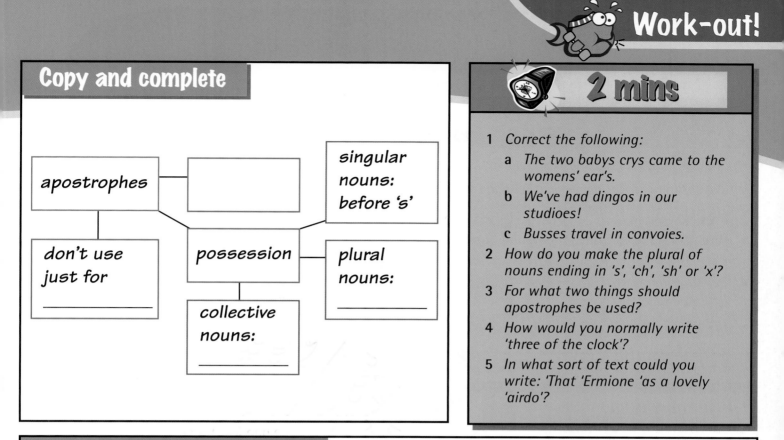

apostrophes

don't use just for

_____

possession

singular nouns: before 's'

plural nouns:

_____

collective nouns:

_____

2 mins

1 Correct the following:
   a The two babys crys came to the womens' ear's.
   b We've had dingos in our studioes!
   c Busses travel in convoies.
2 How do you make the plural of nouns ending in 's', 'ch', 'sh' or 'x'?
3 For what two things should apostrophes be used?
4 How would you normally write 'three of the clock'?
5 In what sort of text could you write: 'That 'Ermione 'as a lovely 'airdo'?

Question and model answer

Correct the following as if you were checking the paragraph at the end of the exam. Look out for mistakes involving apostrophes and plurals.

'Weere sinking! Do'nt panic!' shouted the ships captain. Wed been hit by two torpedo's and both hulls had burst like tomatos. The womens' cabins were evacuated, all the childrens' and babys' toys were bundled out, and the mens' uniforms were changed for oversuit's. The boxs of potato's were taken into the lifeboats, along with all our loafs, and the ship's radioes. Any waives and strays were left behind.

'**We're** sinking! **Don't** panic!' shouted the **ship's** captain. **We'd** been hit by two **torpedoes** and both hulls had burst like **tomatoes**. The **women's** cabins were evacuated, all the **children's** and **babies'** toys were bundled out, and the **men's** uniforms were changed for **oversuits**. The **boxes** of **potatoes** were taken into the lifeboats, along with all our **loaves**, and the ship's **radios**. Any **waifs** and strays were left behind.

Comment

You won't get a test like this in the exam, but you will lose marks if you show that you don't know how to use apostrophes or form plurals correctly. It looks particularly bad when a student (or a greengrocer!) adds an apostrophe just because a word is plural.

Now try this!

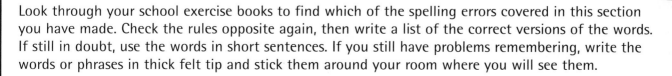

Look through your school exercise books to find which of the spelling errors covered in this section you have made. Check the rules opposite again, then write a list of the correct versions of the words. If still in doubt, use the words in short sentences. If you still have problems remembering, write the words or phrases in thick felt tip and stick them around your room where you will see them.

KS3 Bitesize English

67

Prefixes, suffixes and homophones

1 A prefix *comes at the* start *of a word, changing its meaning:*

- **pre-** do in advance: *prearrange, preview, pre-heat*
- **dis-** (usually) undo: *displace, disengage, disprove*
- **mis-** wrongly: *misspell, mislead, mistake*
- **fore-** before or in front: *foreground, foreman, forearm*
- **ex-** former; out; from: *ex-teacher, expel, exchange*
- **re-** again: *reappear, revisit, remember, reactivate.*

2 *Some* prefixes *form* opposites. *Different words take different prefixes:*

- **in-** : *inattentive, inactive, inappropriate, indistinct, insincere*
- **un-** : *unattractive, unequal, unfair, unfaithful, unappealing*
- **ir-** : *irreplaceable, irrelevant, irreligious, irregular, irresistible*
- **im-** : *impossible, impassable, improper, imprecise, immodest*
- **Note** if the root word begins with the second letter of the prefix, keep both letters: *unnatural, unnoticeable, immodest, irrelevant.*

3 Suffixes *go at the* ends *of words qualifying them:*

- **-ation** used to form a noun from a verb: *invitation, excitation, inspiration*
- **-otion** used in the same way: *commotion, promotion, devotion*
- **-let, -ling** (small): *hamlet, rivulet, gosling, darling*
- **-ess** (female): *manageress, lioness, actress*
- **-able, -ible, -uble**: all convey the idea of something being possible. There are no rules on which to use, but an 'e' is usually dropped before them – *forgiv(e)able*:

> comfortable, passable, believable, fashionable, laughable, drinkable, edible, credible, horrible, terrible, forcible, indelible, divisible, soluble, voluble

4 Homophones *are the spellings your* spellcheck *won't catch – words that sound similar but mean different things:*

- *If you* advise *me I'll take your* advice.
- *What* effect *will it have? Will it* affect *my health?*
- *I've* brought *the friend who* bought *that new CD.*
- *Of* course *he's rather* coarse.
- *The child was* quiet *until* quite *soon after dawn.*
- *I'm* too *tired* to *stay awake until* two *o'clock.*
- *Look over* there *–* they're *eating* their *lunch.*
- *I* accept *that everyone here is useless* except *you.*
- *Wear warm clothes – you'll need them* where *we're going.*

Prefixes go at the start of words, suffixes at the end. Both qualify the meanings of words. Some suffixes form opposites. Homophones are words with similar sounds but different meanings. Your spellcheck won't catch homophone mistakes.

Work-out!

Copy and complete

```
prefixes ── [          ]
         ── qualify
            _____
[          ] ── end of words
```

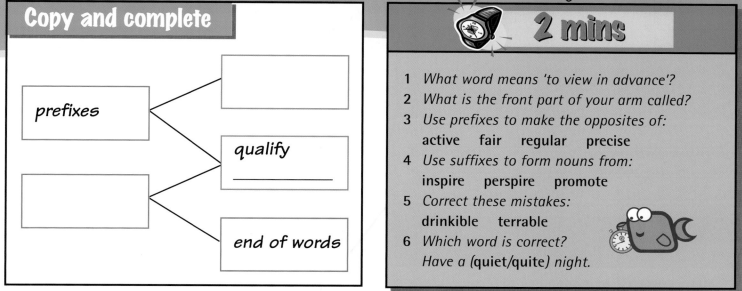

2 mins

1 What word means 'to view in advance'?
2 What is the front part of your arm called?
3 Use prefixes to make the opposites of:
   active   fair   regular   precise
4 Use suffixes to form nouns from:
   inspire   perspire   promote
5 Correct these mistakes:
   drinkible   terrable
6 Which word is correct?
   Have a (quiet/quite) night.

Question and model answer

**Imagine you're checking the paragraph below at the end of your exam.
Find the mistakes.**

The teacher said it was easy to mispell certain words, so James and Gemma wrote them on there forheads. They had always been unattentive in lessons – they found it impossable to concentrate. To they're way of thinking, learning was unatural. Sadly, they had not bought mirrors into the exam, so they were quiet inable to read the spellings. This would effect their marks. 'Theirs no hope,' whispered Gemma. 'Except it – everyone can spell accept us!'

The teacher said it was easy to **misspell** certain words, so James and Gemma wrote them on **their foreheads**. They had always been **inattentive** in lessons – they found it **impossible** to concentrate. To **their** way of thinking, learning was **unnatural**. Sadly, they had not **brought** mirrors into the exam, so they were **quite unable** to read the spellings. This would **affect** their marks. '**There's** no hope,' whispered Gemma. '**Accept** it – everyone can spell **except** us!'

Comment

You won't be tested separately on prefixes, suffixes and homophones, but students often make mistakes with them, and you can impress the examiner by getting them right. If you do make mistakes, you may lose marks.

Now try this!

You will probably not be able to take a dictionary into your SATs exam, but while revising you will find one very valuable for checking spellings. Use one now to check the following. Some are right, others wrong. Write down the full list of correct spellings.

comfortible, passable, believeable, fashionible, laughable, drinkable, unedible, incredable, horible, terrible, forcable, indelible, divisible, insoluble, accomodation, necesary, traveler, beautyful.

Shakespeare's world

1 Shakespeare's plots (stories) and imagery (word pictures) reflect differences between his world and ours in several areas of life:

- class divisions
- the status of women
- travel
- health
- beliefs
- entertainment.

2 England was very class-conscious. This diagram shows the main divisions:

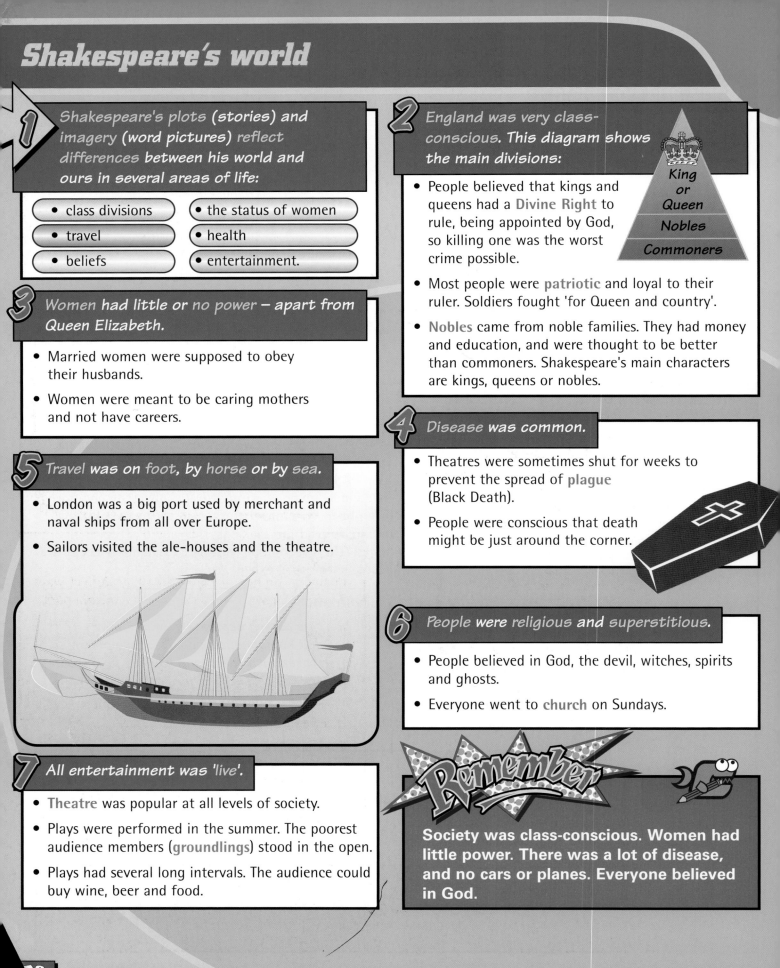

King or Queen
Nobles
Commoners

- People believed that kings and queens had a **Divine Right** to rule, being appointed by God, so killing one was the worst crime possible.
- Most people were **patriotic** and loyal to their ruler. Soldiers fought 'for Queen and country'.
- **Nobles** came from noble families. They had money and education, and were thought to be better than commoners. Shakespeare's main characters are kings, queens or nobles.

3 Women had little or no power – apart from Queen Elizabeth.

- Married women were supposed to obey their husbands.
- Women were meant to be caring mothers and not have careers.

4 Disease was common.

- Theatres were sometimes shut for weeks to prevent the spread of **plague** (Black Death).
- People were conscious that death might be just around the corner.

5 Travel was on foot, by horse or by sea.

- London was a big port used by merchant and naval ships from all over Europe.
- Sailors visited the ale-houses and the theatre.

6 People were religious and superstitious.

- People believed in God, the devil, witches, spirits and ghosts.
- Everyone went to **church** on Sundays.

7 All entertainment was 'live'.

- **Theatre** was popular at all levels of society.
- Plays were performed in the summer. The poorest audience members (**groundlings**) stood in the open.
- Plays had several long intervals. The audience could buy wine, beer and food.

Remember

Society was class-conscious. Women had little power. There was a lot of disease, and no cars or planes. Everyone believed in God.

Work-out!

Copy and complete

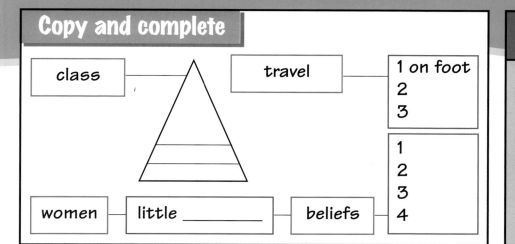

class

travel — 1 on foot / 2 / 3

1 / 2 / 3 / 4

women — little _____ — beliefs — 4

2 mins

Shakespeare is coming to visit you for a week.
Referring to the list of differences opposite, list six things that you would need to explain to him about modern life.

Question and model answer

In this passage from *The Tempest*, **the drunken butler Stephano finds Caliban and Trinculo hiding, their legs sticking out from under a coat. Comment on how it reflects differences between our world and Shakespeare's.**

Stephano: What's the matter? Have we devils here? Do you put tricks upon's with savages and men of Ind, ha? I have not scaped drowning to be afeard now of your four legs; for it hath been said, 'As proper a man as ever went on four legs cannot make him give ground.'...
Caliban: The spirit torments me; Oh!
Stephano: This is some monster of the isle with four legs, who hath got, as I take it, an ague. Where the devil should he learn our language? I will give him some relief, if it be but for that. If I can recover him and keep him tame and get to Naples with him, he's a present for any emperor that ever trod on neat's leather. (Act 2, Scene 2)

1 Stephano has been shipwrecked, a common occurrence at this time, but has 'scaped drowning'.
2 Hearing Caliban's voice and seeing four legs, he thinks devils are tricking him 'with savages and men of Ind[ia]'. This reflects the beliefs of the time, as does Calibans fear of spirits.
3 Stephano's mention of 'ague' (fever) reflects how common sickness was.
4 This was a time of exploration, when sailors brought back tails of monsters and people believed them. Stephano thinks he has found a monster, and hopes to make money from it.
5 Stephano's stupidity reflects the fact he is a commoner. not a noble.

Comments

1 *Understands the context of the play.*
2 *Understands the beliefs of the time.*
3 *Knowledge of social context - sickness.*
4 *Knowledge of world events in Shakespeare's time and their influence.*
5 *Understands the class system.*

Now try this!

Comment on how the following lines reflect ways in which Shakespeare's world differed from ours.

Prospero:
... graves at my command
Have waked their sleepers, oped, and let 'em forth
By my so potent art. But this rough magic
I here abjure. (*abjure*: renounce, give up)
(*The Tempest*, Act 5, Scene 1)

King Richard:
Fight, gentlemen of England! Fight, bold yeomen!
Draw, archers, draw your arrows to the head!
Spur your proud horses hard, and ride in blood!
(*Richard III*, Act 5, Scene 3)

Claudio:
Sweet prince, you learn me noble thankfulness.
There Leonata, take her back again:
Give not this rotten orange to your friend;
She's but the sign and semblance of her honour.
(*Much Ado about Nothing*, Act 4, Scene 1)

History, comedy, tragedy

1 Shakespeare wrote three main types of play: *histories, comedies* and *tragedies.*

For example: • *Richard III* is a history. • *Much Ado about Nothing* is a comedy. • *Macbeth* is a tragedy.

2 Each type of play has different characteristics.

Histories	Comedies	Tragedies
Based on real people and events.	Misunderstandings (especially about love) which are eventually sorted out.	Conflict (sometimes battle), dishonesty and revenge.
Main themes are kingship, loyalty, patriotism and the security of the social order.	Humour (including puns), tricks and practical jokes. Disguises, including women dressed as men.	A basically noble and brave hero grows as a character, then dies.
There is a threat to the kingdom. After a battle, the King is reaffirmed as the head of a peaceful kingdom.	People fall in love and eventually get married. Happy ending. In comedies like *The Tempest*, this maybe achieved magically and by forgiveness.	Hero's death caused by fate, often coupled with a personal weakness or error.

3 All three types of play can be understood using the STAR formula:

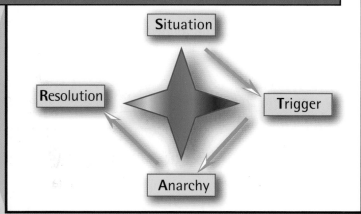

4 These four words refer to stages of any Shakespeare play:

- **Situation**: how things are at the start of the play (e.g. the kingdom is unsettled).
- **Trigger**: the event that sparks the play's main action (e.g. Prospero is exiled).
- **Anarchy**: the stage of most confusion and disorder (e.g. a battle).
- **Resolution**: peace and order restored (end of confusion; marriages, or kingdom peacefully united under a good king).

HELP! Don't be confused by overlaps between the three types of play. Both history and tragedy include some humour, and comedies can contain a serious message - especially 'Problem' comedies such as *The Tempest*. All types can include trickery, but in comedy it is playful.

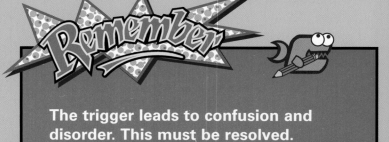

The trigger leads to confusion and disorder. This must be resolved.

Copy and complete

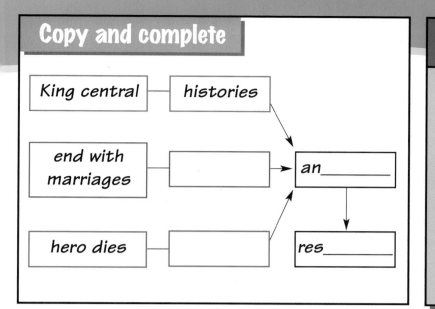

King central	—	histories
end with marriages		
hero dies		

an_____

res_____

Answer for the play you are studying.

1 Is it based on real people and events?
2 Does it contain conflict and deaths?
3 Is its main character a king from start to finish?
4 Does the main character die?
5 Does anyone wear a disguise?
6 What is the main trigger to the action?
7 What form does the 'anarchy' (disorder) take?
8 How is the play resolved at the end?

Question and model answer

Discuss the relationship of the characters in this extract from *The Tempest* and how the extract shows that the play is a comedy.

Miranda: ... I am your wife, if you will marry me;
If not, I'll die your maid. To be your fellow
You may deny me; but I'll be your servant,
Whether you will or no.

Ferdinand: My mistress, dearest;
And I thus humble ever.

Miranda: My husband, then?

Ferdinand: Ay, with a heart as willing
As bondage e'er of freedom: here's my hand.

Miranda: And mine, with my heart in't; and now farewell
Till half an hour hence.

Ferdinand: A thousand thousand!

1 All Shakespeare comedies include love between noble characters. Miranda says she will marry Ferdinand or die, and her feelings are matched by his. Their nobility is shown by their mutual respect, and by Miranda's saying that she will remain a maid if necessary. This is a pun: 'maid' means both a virgin and a servant.

2 At first, neither lover is sure of the other's love. Miranda is especially uncertain ('if you will marry ...'). This shows that they have only just fallen in love. The extreme language also show this: Miranda's claim that she would be Ferdinand's servant to be with him, and Ferdinand's exaggerated farewell.

3 When Ferdinand says that he is as willing to marry Miranda as a man in bondage is to be free, this reflects his situation too: he is being tested by Miranda's father, who has enslaved him. This kind of well-meaning trick is found in comedies.

Comments

This answer shows:

• ability to work out the meaning without necessarily understanding every word

• understanding of the key features of Shakespearean comedy

• ability to relate the details of this play's plot to Shakespearean comedy generally.

Now try this!

Use the STAR formula to write four short paragraphs (one for each letter) about the play you are studying. (See page 74, 76 or 78 if you need to remind yourself of the plot.) Write a final paragraph explaining what features make it a history, a comedy or a tragedy.

Plot and themes in a tragedy

1 The **plot** (story) **of a tragedy fits perfectly into the STAR formula shown on page 72. The resolution comes with the death of the tragic hero.**

- Here is the plot of *Macbeth* – a typical tragedy – split into the **play's** five **Acts**.

ACT 1

The Witches predict that Macbeth will be Thane (Lord) of Cawdor, then King, and Banquo's descendants will be kings.

King Duncan makes Macbeth Thane of Cawdor. Lady Macbeth persuades Macbeth to murder Duncan so he can become King right away.

ACT 2

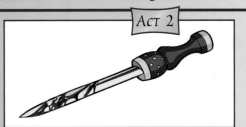

Macbeth murders Duncan in his sleep. Duncan's sons flee.

ACT 3

Macbeth is crowned and has Banquo killed. Banquo's son escapes. Banquo's ghost scares Macbeth at a banquet.

ACT 4

The Witches' spirits tell Macbeth to beware Macduff but that he is safe until Birnam Wood comes to Dunsinane. He has Macduff's family killed.

ACT 5

Malcolm

Duncan's son Malcolm leads an army against Macbeth at Dunsinane, using trees from Birnam Wood as camouflage. Lady Macbeth kills herself. Macduff fights and kills Macbeth. Malcolm becomes king.

2 **Themes are the main ideas the play explores. Some important themes of Macbeth are:**

- **Evil** – are the Witches to blame, or Macbeth?

- **Courage** – Macbeth worries about being 'a real man'.

- **Deception** – Macbeth pretends he is innocent; the Witches trick him.

- **Order and disorder** – a bad king creates disorder; a good one creates order.

Remember

Work out how your scenes fit into the play – what leads up to them, and what they lead to.

Copy and complete

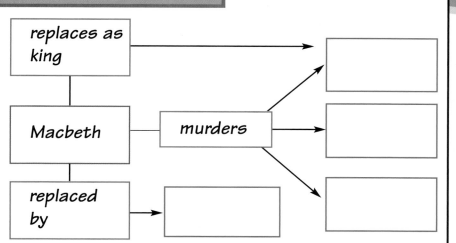

replaces as king →

Macbeth — murders →

replaced by →

2 mins

1 Who says Macbeth will be king?
2 What do Duncan's sons do after his murder?
3 Why must Banquo's son escape?
4 Who is Macbeth warned against?
5 Who does Lady Macbeth kill?
6 Name four themes of 'Macbeth'.

Question and model answer

How does the following passage fit into the plot and reflect the play's themes?

Macbeth: *Avaunt! and quit my sight! Let the earth hide thee!*
                  Thy bones are marrowless, thy blood is cold;
                  Thou hast no speculation in those eyes
                  Which thou dost glare with.

Lady Macbeth: *Think of this, good peers,*
                  But as a thing of custom: 'tis no other;
                  Only it spoils the pleasure of the time.

Macbeth: *What man dare, I dare …*

1 This is in Act 3, Scene 4. Macbeth has murdered Duncan and become King. To make his position secure he has had Banquo murdered. Macbeth and his wife are holding a banquet to celebrate Macbeth being crowned, but Banquo's ghost appears to him and terrifies him. Lady Macbeth pretends his behaviour is normal, but people do start to suspect.

2 The theme of evil is reflected by the ghost, suggesting the evil of Banquo's murder. The ghost itself may not be evil, but it is a supernatural being, like the spirits later called up by the evil Witches.

3 The theme of courage is explored in Macbeth's fear, and in his claim that he will face any normal danger ('What man dare …'). He means he is as brave as any man.

4 The theme of deception is shown in Lady Macbeth pretending to the guests that everything is normal ('a thing of custom').

5 Macbeth is a bad king, and his rule creates disorder. This is shown by the confusion that his 'seeing' the ghost creates among his guests.

Comments

This answer shows:

- understanding of context (how the passage fits into the play) – both what has led up to this scene and its immediate consequences

- ability to relate the passage to the themes of the play

- understanding of the language, shown by reference to the text, with short quotations.

Now try this!

Open a copy of *Macbeth* at random and read the page in front of you. Jot down where in the plot you think it is, what has led up to it, and what happens next. Also try to find at least one theme that it suggests. Then check by looking back and forwards from this page. To check your recall of themes, look back to the list opposite.

Plot and themes in a comedy

1 Get to know the play's **plot** (story) to understand how the scenes you're studying fit in.

- Here is the plot of *Much Ado About Nothing*, divided into the five **Acts** of the play.

Act 1

Don Pedro, Benedick and Claudio return from war. Benedick and Beatrice tease each other as usual. Claudio falls in love with Hero. Don Pedro says he'll woo her for him. Don Pedro's wicked brother Don John plans to use this against Claudio.

Act 2

Don John tells Claudio that Don Pedro intends to marry Hero himself. But Don Pedro announces that he has arranged her marriage to Claudio. Don Pedro decides to pair off Benedick and Beatrice. Don John plots to foil Claudio's marriage. Don Pedro, Claudio and Leonato trick Benedick into believing Beatrice loves him.

> Don Pedro's stolen Hero!

Act 3

Beatrice is tricked into thinking Benedick loves her. Don John pays Borachio to woo Margaret at Hero's window. Claudio and Don Pedro think Hero has a lover. Claudio vows to shame her. The constables hear Borachio boasting to Conrade and arrests them both.

Act 4

Claudio publicly shames Hero. She faints and he leaves. Friar Francis pleads her innocence and plans to change Claudio's heart by making him think she's dead. Benedick declares his love to Beatrice. She tells him to prove it by killing Claudio.

> Kill Claudio!

Act 5

Claudio is challenged – by Leonato, then Benedick. Borachio confesses to Don Pedro and Claudio that Hero was innocent. Claudio agrees to sing a tribute at her grave and marry her cousin. The 'cousin' turns out to be Hero. Beatrice agrees to marry Benedick. The play ends with a happy dance.

2 **Themes** are the main ideas a play explores. Some themes of Much Ado About Nothing are:

- **Love** – it takes people by surprise and can bring tears before joy.

- **Deception** – trickery, whether for good or bad motives, causes chaos.

- **Honour** – in seeking to avoid dishonour, Claudio dishonours Hero and her family.

- **Renewal** – the friendship between Benedick and Claudio, Claudio's faith in Hero, and Hero's honour are all restored.

Remember

Work out how your scenes fit into the play. See how the comedy nearly turns to tragedy. Understand the importance of Don John as a 'trigger'.

Copy and complete

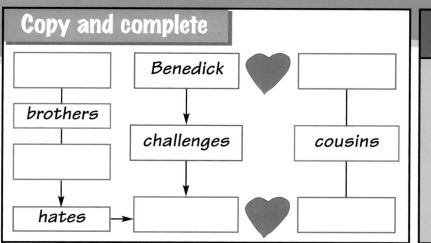

1 Who pretends to dislike Beatrice?
2 Who is the chief villain?
3 Who woos Hero?
4 Who is publicly shamed?
5 Who says 'Kill Claudio'?
6 Who pretends to be Hero?
7 How is Borachio found out?
8 Who is at the top of the social ladder?

Question and model answer

How does the following passage fit into the plot of the play and reflect the play's themes?

Beatrice:	*Will you not eat your word?*
Benedick:	*With no sauce that can be devised to it. I protest I love thee.*
Beatrice:	*Why then, God forgive me!*
Benedick:	*What offence, sweet Beatrice?*
Beatrice:	*You have stayed me in a happy hour. I was about to protest I loved you.*
Benedick:	*And do it with all thy heart.*
Beatrice:	*I love you with so much of my heart that none is left to protest.*
Benedick:	*Come, bid me do anything for thee.*
Beatrice:	*Kill Claudio!*
Benedick:	*Ha, not for the wide world!*

1 This passage, in Act 4, Scene 1, seems to show the comedy on the verge of turning to tragedy. The light-heartedness of Act 1 is threatened. Don John, the Prince's wicked brother, has tricked Claudio into believing that Claudio's bride-to-be, Hero, has been unfaithful. Claudio has therefore shamed her by denouncing her at their wedding. Hero's cousin Beatrice believes she is innocent and wants Benedick to take revenge on Claudio.

2 The passage reflects the theme of surprise love. Earlier in the play, the couple enjoyed insulting each other. Now they are reluctant to admit to being in love. Beatrice says it is fortunate for her ('a happy hour') that Benedick has admitted it first. Given their past, she can hardly believe that he loves her. She fears he will go back on what he says ('Will you not eat your word?'). His response ('With no sauce ...') is typical of the word-play between them, but now it is loving, not teasing. When he refuses to kill Claudio, she takes it as proof that he does not love her after all.

3 Beatrice's demand creates dramatic tension: Benedick must choose between her and his friendship with Claudio. For both Benedick and Beatrice, there is honour at stake – an important thing in Shakespeare's time. Beatrice herself is dishonoured by the slur on her cousin's character. It would also dishonour Benedick to refuse Beatrice's request.

Comments

This answer shows:

- **understanding of how the passage fits into the play – both what has led up to this scene and how it creates dramatic tension which must be resolved**
- **ability to relate the passage to the play's themes (especially love and honour)**
- **understanding of the language, shown by reference to the text.**

Now try this!

Open a copy of *Much Ado About Nothing* at random and read the page in front of you. Jot down where in the plot you think it is, what has led up to it, and what happens next. Also try to find at least one theme that it suggests. Then check by looking back and forward from this page. To check your recall of themes, look back to the list opposite.

Plot and themes in a history

1 All Shakespeare's history plays focus on a king. He may be heroic and noble, as in Henry V, or evil and scheming, as in Richard III.

2 Compare the plots of these two plays, shown below. See how both fit the STAR formula (see page 72). How do they differ? What do they have in common?

Richard III

Act 1

Richard wants to be King. He woos Anne – whose husband he killed. He slanders Queen Elizabeth and has his brother Clarence murdered.

Act 2

Richard feigns friendship with Elizabeth. King Edward dies. Richard and Buckingham imprison Grey and Rivers. Queen tries to protect her sons from Richard.

Act 3

Richard lures the princes into the Tower. Hastings is beheaded for not supporting him. Richard has Buckingham argue his claim to the throne, then refuses it for show.

Act 4 Richard seizes throne. Buckingham reluctant to murder the princes. Richard has them killed. War looms. Richard is cursed by Margaret, Elizabeth and his own mother. He distrusts and threatens Stanley.

Act 5 Richard executes Buckingham. Before Battle of Bosworth, the ghosts of Richard's victims curse him and bless Richmond. Richard slain in battle by Richmond – who becomes King.

Henry V

Act 1

Henry decides to claim the French throne. The Dauphin sends him an insulting present – tennis balls.

Act 2 Henry condemns three traitors and declares war on France.

Act 3

War in France. English sick, hungry, outnumbered, but Henry won't surrender.

Act 4 Before battle of Agincourt, Henry wanders in disguise talking to his men.

Act 5

Henry negotiates treaty with France – and marriage to French princess Katharine.

Copy and complete

Henry or Richard?

. . . . leads England to victory.

. . . . divides England.

. . . . is honest and loyal.

. . . . is treacherous.

. . . . is alive at the end.

. . . . dies at the end.

2 mins

1 Which throne does Henry claim?
2 Which throne does Richard claim?
3 Who does Henry condemn in Act 2?
4 Who does Richard murder in Act 1?
5 How does Henry V end ?
6 How does Richard III end?

Question and model answer

How does the following passage from Richard III fit into the plot and reflect the play's themes?

1st Murderer: *Thy brother's love, our duty, and thy faults*
Provoke us hither now to slaughter thee.

Clarence: *O, if you love my brother, hate not me:*
I am his brother, and I love him well.
If you are hir'd for meed, go back again,
And I will send you to my brother Gloucester,
Who shall reward you better for my life
Than Edward will for tidings of my death.

2nd Murderer: *You are deceiv'd: your brother Gloucester hates you.*

Clarence: *O no, he loves me, and he holds me dear;*
Go you to him from me.

1st Murderer: *Ay, so we will.*

meed: unlawful profit

1 Here, in Act 1, scene 4, Clarence pleads with two murderers sent by his younger brother Richard (Gloucester) to kill him.

2 A major theme is kingship. Richard will do anything to become King. But Clarence thinks King Edward has sent the murderers. Earlier he argues that the commandment of Christ, 'King of Kings', outweighs Edward's 'command'.

3 The passage also relates to loyalty. Clarence's loyalty to Edward and Richard will be rewarded by death. The 1st Murderer insists that he is driven by 'duty' (to the King).

4 The theme of power is clearly present. Richard will stop at nothing to gain power. Clarence is in the murderers' power and has only the power of persuasion to save himself.

5 Richard deceives Clarence into believing in his love: 'he holds me dear'. It is ironic when Clarence tells the murderers to go to Richard. Even the 1st Murderer's reply is deceptive: they will go when Clarence is dead.

Comments

This answer shows:

- *understanding of context (how the passage fits into the play) – both what has led up to this scene and how it will be resolved;*

- *ability to relate the passage to the themes of the play;*

- *understanding of the language, shown by reference to the text.*

Now try this!

Open a copy of *Henry V* or *Richard III* at random and read the page in front of you. Jot down where in the plot you think it is, what has led up to it, and what happens next. Also try to find at least one theme that it suggests. Then check by looking back and forwards from this page. To check your recall of themes, look back to the list opposite.

Characterisation in a tragedy

1 The central character in a *tragedy* is brought low by a mixture of *fate* and his own *flaws*. Taking *Macbeth* as our example, we see he is the play's *tragic hero*.

- Lady Macbeth is important, but she almost disappears after Act 3.
- Macbeth is the play's central character.

2 See how Macbeth *relates to* the other characters.

Macduff
Opposes Macbeth. Brave, honest, loyal, but leaves family in danger. Kills Macbeth in revenge, and for Scotland.

Lady Macduff
Brave wife murdered with her children by Macbeth.

Duncan
Generous king. Mistakenly trusts Macbeth.

Witches
Evil hags who trick with half-truths.

Macbeth
Man of action. Has a conscience but is ambitious. Lets himself be talked into murder by his wife calling him a coward. Trusts the Witches too much. Becomes treacherous and brutal but dies bravely.

Lady Macbeth
Ambitious, ruthless, manipulative, two-faced. Tries to make Macbeth act tough but cracks up herself.

Banquo
Macbeth's friend and fellow general. Good, but suspects Macbeth and does nothing. Murdered by him.

Malcolm
Duncan's son. More cautious, clever. Will make a good king.

3 Always base what you say about characters on the *evidence* of the play.

Macbeth: *... He's here in double trust:*
First, as I am his kinsman and his subject,
Strong both against the deed; then, as his host,
Who should against his murderer shut the door,
Not bear the knife myself. Besides, this Duncan
Hath borne his faculties so meek, hath been
So clear in his great office, that his virtues
Will plead like angels, trumpet-tongued, against
The deep damnation of his taking off.
(Act 1, Scene 7)

- This shows that at this point, Macbeth wants to avoid evil. He respects the bonds of family, hospitality and loyalty to his king (he is Duncan's 'kinsman', 'host' and 'subject'). Moreover, he feels it would be a great sin to kill so 'meek' and virtuous a man. But 60 lines on, his wife has changed his mind: he lacks the moral strength to resist evil.

Remember

Think about character relationships. Base your character analysis on the text. Characters develop as the play progresses.

Copy and complete

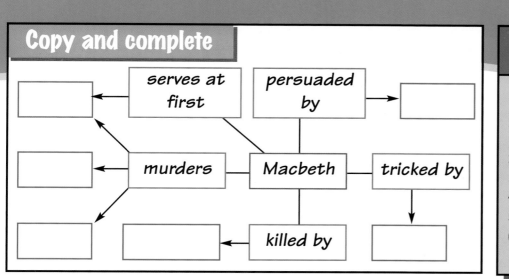

	serves at first	persuaded by	
murders	Macbeth	tricked by
	killed by	

1 Which king is too trusting?
2 Who suspects but does nothing?
3 Who persuades Macbeth to murder?
4 Whose family is murdered?
5 Who is cautious and clever?
6 What are Macbeth's reasons for not murdering Duncan?

Question and model answer

Read Macbeth's speech below (from Act 4, Scene 1) and comment on how he has changed since the one given opposite.

The flighty purpose never is o'ertook

Unless the deed go with it; from this moment

The very firstlings of my heart shall be

The firstlings of my hand. And even now,

To crown my thoughts with acts, be it thought and done:

The castle of Macduff I will surprise;

Seize upon Fife; give to the edge of the sword

His wife, his babes, and all unfortunate souls

That trace him in his line. No boasting like a fool;

This deed I'll do before this purpose cool.

1 In Act 1, Scene 7, Macbeth's ambition struggles with his morality. He thinks hard about whether he should kill Duncan, and finds good reasons for not doing it. In the second extract he has almost abandoned morality, and thinks only of staying King.

2 He says that you can never act as quickly as you intend unless you do a deed the moment you think of it. In Act 1, he worries about what to do; here he declares that from now on he will act immediately on what comes into his heart ('the firstlings of my heart').

3 To prove his point he makes an instant decision – to murder Macduff's family. He does not worry whether they deserve it. He now thinks that action is above thought: it is thought's 'crown'. His new dynamic mood shows in his language. In the first extract he used an elaborate image for Duncan's virtues, 'like angels, trumpet-tongued', but in the second the simple language is that of a man of action. The final rhyming couplet suggests no-nonsense determination.

Comments

1 Neatly sums up how Macbeth's attitude has changed. Identifies the sense of moral struggle – and that Macbeth has given up on it.

2 Clear and relevant explanation of Macbeth's sentiments in the second extract and how they compare with those of the first. Appropriate use of a short quote.

3 Explanation of Macbeth's decision linked to analysis of how the language of the extracts reflects the change in Macbeth. Correct use of literary terms: image and rhyming couplet.

This is a level 7 or 8 answer. Level 5 or 6 might not make such a clear comparison, and might identify only one change in Macbeth – either moral or from thought to action. It would show less understanding of how Shakespeare's language reflects the changes.

Now try this!

Compare Macbeth's speech given above with the speech he makes on hearing of his wife's death (Act 5, Scene 5, lines 17–28: 'She should have died hereafter ... Signifying nothing'). Think especially about his mood and language.

Characterisation in a comedy

1 In comedies it is important to understand relationships – including family ties, friendships, loves and hates. See the character map below from Much Ado About Nothing.

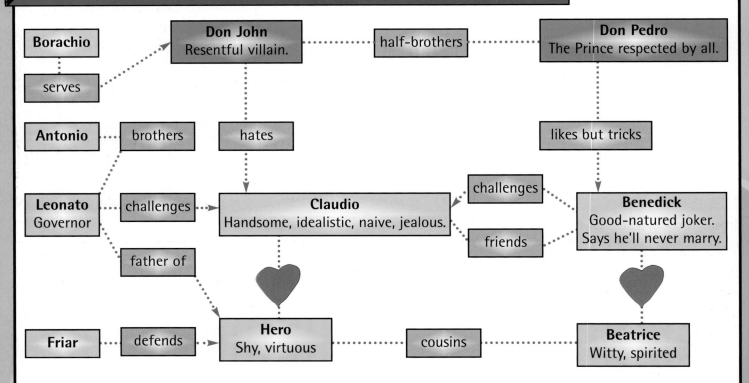

2 Always base what you say about characters on the *evidence* of the play.

Claudio: There, Leonato, take her back again.
Give not this rotten orange to your friend;
She's but the sign and semblance of her honour.
Behold how like a maid she blushes here!
O, what authority and show of truth
Can cunning sin cover itself withal!
Comes not that blood as modest evidence
To witness simple virtue? Would you not swear,
All you that see her, that she were a maid,
By these exterior shows? But she is none.

(Act 4, Scene 1)

- Claudio's bitter accusation shows his disappointment in Hero. Yet he is cruel to let her think he is about to marry her, then shame her. It is also a jealous misjudgement to see her blushes as trickery when he has so quickly believed the false evidence against her.

Remember

Think about the characters' relationships and how they develop, and about how the characters trick each other.

Copy and complete

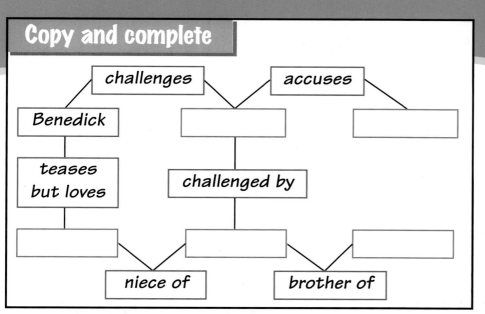

challenges   accuses

Benedick

teases but loves

challenged by

niece of   brother of

Who is ...

1 resentful and scheming?
2 a determined bachelor?
3 too shocked and shy to speak?
4 thirsty for revenge?
5 quick to believe false proof?
6 keen to prove his love?
7 an angry father?

Question and model answer

Read the passage below (from Act 5 scene 1) and comment on what it shows about Claudio's character relative to the speech given opposite.

Leonato: Here stand a pair of honourable men –
              A third is fled – that had a hand in it.
              I thank you, Princes, for my daughter's death;
              Record it with your high and worthy deeds;
              'Twas bravely done, if you bethink you of it.

Claudio: I know not how to pray your patience,
              Yet I must speak. Choose your revenge yourself,
              Impose me to what penance your invention
              Can lay upon my sin; yet sinn'd I not
              But in my mistaking.

1 In the first passage, Claudio shows he can be bitter, and even cruel, when he feels himself to be wronged. He seems proud and unforgiving.

2 In the second passage, Leonato bitterly taunts both Claudio and Don Pedro, accusing them of killing Hero. His ironic thanks and praise are meant to sting. Yet Claudio, now that he realises his own fault, endures these taunts. He does not respond in kind. Even if he was quick to condemn Hero, he is now quick to admit his guilt and to put himself at Leonato's mercy. He wants to do 'penance' for his 'sin'.

3 However, not everyone would agree with Claudio's claim, 'I sinn'd not/ But in mistaking'. This shows that while he accepts his guilt, he blames it on his being tricked. He does not admit to any guilt in being so ready to doubt Hero's innocence without even asking her to defend herself.

Comments

1 Summarises what the first speech shows, identifying why Claudio is cruel.

2 Shows understanding of the insult offered by Leonato's speech – and therefore what it reveals about Claudio when he humbly accepts it.

3 Identifies what Claudio's claim suggests: he only partly accepts blame.

This answer ranks as a level 7 or 8. It shows understanding of how Claudio's character is revealed by his response to Leonato, and the limits on Claudio's acceptance of guilt.

Now try this!

Compare Claudio's speech with Act 2, Scene 1, lines 160–70 ('Thus answer I ...'), when he thinks that Don Pedro has wooed Hero for himself. How does this misunderstanding prepare us for Claudio's later behaviour?

Characterisation in a history

1 In histories, the main character is always a king.

- Henry V is an example of a good king, Richard III an example of a bad king.

2 Shakespeare presents Richard III as an evil man whose kingship makes England unstable, unsafe and unhappy. Look at his character traits below, and see how they are revealed by the evidence of the play. He is in most ways the opposite of Shakespeare's ideal king.

Unpredictable
Suddenly turns on Hastings: 'Thou art a traitor/ Off with his head! (Act 3, Scene 4)

Unjust
Orders the murder of innocent people (such as the Princes) and even his own supporters (such as Buckingham, Act 5, Scene 1).

Resentful
because his deformity makes him unattractive to women (Act 1, Scene 1).

Arch-deceiver
Pretends to love Anne, woos her, and revels in his deception (end of Act 1, Scene 2). Pretends to be his brother Clarence's protector (Act 1, Scene 1), plots with Buckingham to deceive the Mayor (Act 3, Scene 5), and pretends to refuse the crown out of humility (end of Act 3).

Heartless
Forces himself on Anne, whose husband he has murdered, and then has her murdered in turn. Also has his nephews the Princes murdered in the Tower (Act 4, Scene 3).

Godless
He never repents. Richmond calls him 'God's enemy' (Act 5, Scene 3).

Villain
by choice: '... since I cannot prove a lover ... I am determined to prove a villain' (Act 1, Scene 1).

Prefers war
to peace. See his opening soliloquy (Act 1, Scene 1). Starts civil war.

3 The notes above sum up Richard's character, but always base your assessment on the text.

Richard: I, that am curtail'd of this fair proportion,
Cheated of feature by dissembling nature,
Deformed, unfinish'd, sent before my time
Into this breathing world, scarce half made up,
And that so lamely and unfashionable
That dogs bark at me as I halt by them;
Why, I, in this weak piping time of peace,
Have no delight to pass away the time,
Unless to spy my shadow in the sun
And descant on mine own deformity.

- This shows that Richard bitterly resents his deformity, and feels he has been cheated by nature. He focuses on being rejected because of his appearance, rather than his character. He gives this as a reason for his preferring war to peace, since he cannot pursue love like other men.

Remember

The King is the main character. Henry V is an ideal king, merciful, tough and inspiring. Richard III is the opposite, an evil schemer who is finally replaced as King.

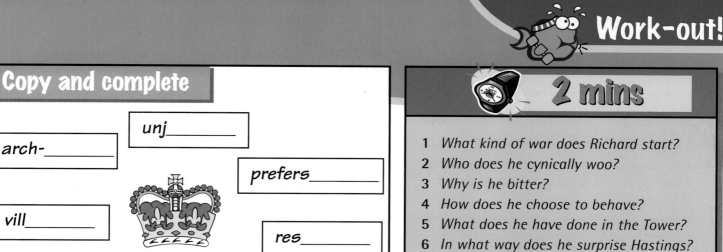
Copy and complete

arch-_____

unj_____

prefers_____

vill_____

res_____

Richard III

God_____

heart____

unpre_____

2 mins

1 What kind of war does Richard start?
2 Who does he cynically woo?
3 Why is he bitter?
4 How does he choose to behave?
5 What does he have done in the Tower?
6 In what way does he surprise Hastings?
7 What does Richmond call him?
8 Who is Clarence?

Question and model answer

The night before battle, Richard is visited by the ghosts of those he has murdered. How does his speech on awaking reflect his character and mood, compared with the one opposite?

Richard: *Give me another horse: bind up my wounds.*
Have mercy, Jesu! - Soft! I did but dream.
O coward conscience, how dost thou afflict me!
The lights burn blue. It is now dead midnight.
Cold fearful drops stand on my trembling flesh.
What do I fear? Myself? There's none else by:
Richard loves Richard; that is, I am I.
Is there a murderer here? No. Yes, I am:
Then fly. What, from myself? Great reason why:
Lest I revenge. What, myself upon myself?
Alack. I love myself. Wherefore? For any good
That I myself have done unto myself?
O, no! alas, I rather hate myself
For hateful deeds committed by myself!
I am a villain: yet I lie. I am not.
Fool, of thyself speak well: fool, do not flatter.
(Act 5, Scene 3)

1 In the first speech Richard is bitter but calmly self-confident. He complains about nature's treatment of him and goes on to embrace villainy. In the second he is tormented by fear.

2 The first few words of the second speech are spoken while he is half asleep: he thinks he is in battle. Hence, his uncharacteristic appeal to Jesus comes from his unconscious mind.

3 His disturbed state shows not only in the ideas expressed, but in the broken rhythms, short sentences and contradictions ('I am a villain: yet I lie. I am not.')

4 He is afraid, yet scorns fear and tries to persuade himself that he should not fear himself. However, he is highly confused and admits to having done 'hateful deeds'.

Comments

1 Sums up the contrast between the speeches.
2 Shows ability to analyse the text in close detail.
3 Shows an awareness of how style reflects content.
4 Reveals an understanding of the contradictions in Richard's character.

This is a level 7 answer because it 'reads between the lines', interpreting the text, and analyses the language used, not just the ideas.

Now try this!

Compare Richard's speech above with his cynical wooing of Anne in Act 1, Scene 2, and especially his vain self-congratulation, line 232 ('Was ever woman in this humour woo'd?') to the end of the scene.

Shakespeare: writing in role

1 You may be asked to write *in role* as a Shakespeare character.

- This means putting yourself in the place of a character and writing as if you were that character.

2 Writing in role can be *fun*. It is also a chance to show how well you *know* the play and *understand* the set passages.

Here are some hints:

- Try to **imagine** what the character could be thinking and feeling.
- Base your ideas on the **evidence** of the play.
- You could give a **flavour** of the period by using occasional words or phrases from the set passages. But don't try to write like Shakespeare (unless you're a genius).
- Use an appropriate **tone** (see page 24); for example, serious, light-hearted, angry.
- Show that you know the whole play, by all means. But **focus** on the set extracts.

3 You will be basing what you write on *two* extracts. For example:

- You could be asked to write from the position of a character in the second extract, **looking back** on how things were at the time of the first.
- You could be asked to write about how you (the character) feel about one or more **other characters**.

4 You might, for example, begin like this:

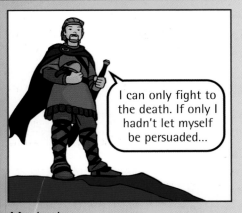

Macbeth
(Act 1, Scene 7; Act 5, Scene 5)

Much Ado About Nothing
(Act 1, Scene 1; Act 3, Scene 2)

Richard III
(Act 1, Scene 2)

HELP! You can speculate about what a character's hopes and fears **might** be, but don't just make things up. Don't give Richard a long-lost aunty if he hasn't got one in the play. (He hasn't!)

Remember

Imagine yourself in the character's situation, using evidence from both extracts.

Copy and complete

Imagine _____ .

Use the evidence of _____ .

Give a flavour of_____ .

Write in an appropriate _____ .

Focus on the_____ .

2 mins

1 How many extracts should you focus on?
2 In writing style, what are **serious, light-hearted** and **angry** examples of?
3 Who might say the lines given below, and when (answer for the play you're studying):
   a **Macbeth:** 'It's no wonder my wife's falling apart. She used to be so strong ...'
   b **Much Ado About Nothing:** 'I used to love teasing Beatrice, but now ...'
   c **The Tempest:** 'I'm going to miss Ariel when I get home ...'
   d **Richard III:** 'This is what I deserve for helping a villain!'

Question and model answer

In *Much Ado About Nothing*, Claudio is tricked into believing that his bride-to-be, Hero, has been unfaithful to him. He resolves to give her up, and to do this when it will shame her the most – at the altar on their wedding day. He does this and is backed up by Don Pedro and Don John. She faints in grief and shock.
If you have a copy of the play, read Act 4, scene 1, up to [*Hero swoons.*] (line 109).

Imagine you are Hero. Write about how you feel the next day.

I think my heart will burst. I relive that moment in the church again and again. I thought that today I'd be happily married to the finest man in Messina, starting a new life with the man I loved. Instead my life is ruined. Innocent as I am, everyone will believe Claudio – that I'm 'a rotten orange'. My family is shamed for ever. After all, Don Pedro and Don John themselves accused me – in front of everyone. It could kill my poor father. The last thing I heard before I passed out was him saying 'Hath no man's dagger here a point for me?' I think that was what finally overcame me. Even he believed in my guilt – in a way that hurts the most. Perhaps if I'd defended myself better ... But I was in a state of shock. Was Claudio tricked, or did he always mean to raise my hopes and dash them? Perhaps I'll never know.

Now try this!

Read the two passages that you are studying. Choose a character who is in both and write a diary entry for that character saying how they feel about their situation. You could include reflections on what has happened so far, regrets, hopes and fears.

Comment

This answer is shorter than you should write, but it shows a grasp of the situation and of what Hero might feel: hurt, shame, a sense of betrayal, and complete bafflement. It shows understanding of the Elizabethan context – people would probably believe the man, not the woman. It makes good use of short quotes. It also suggests personal interpretation based on the evidence – notably that Hero might well have been most wounded by her father's reaction, and that she does not defend herself very well.

Shakespeare's language

1 To appreciate Shakespeare's language you need to know about his use of:

- verse and prose
- vocabulary
- imagery
- sound effects.

2 **Blank verse** is what Shakespeare's characters usually speak.

- It is **unrhymed** (blank) **poetry** in which most lines have **five pairs of syllables**. In each pair, there is **emphasis** on the **second** syllable:

  The **te**nder **love** I **bear** your **Grace**, my **lord**

- Tap out the **rhythm**. When Shakespeare varies this it subtly affects mood and meaning:

  Talk'st **thou** to **me** of **ifs**! Thou **art** a **trai**tor

- Shakespeare emphasises traitor by adding an extra syllable, because King Richard is calling Hastings one and it is a very serious accusation.

3 **Prose** (writing not in verse) is mostly used:

- by **commoners** (non-nobles; e.g. Stephano and Trinculo)
- by anyone who has gone **mad** (e.g. Lady Macbeth)

4 **Vocabulary** refers to the choice of words.

- Shakespeare uses words to suit the **character**, **mood** and **purpose**.
- In the lines quoted under point 2, above, Richard uses short, punchy words to express his bitter accusation of Hastings in a no-nonsense style.

5 **Imagery** means the use of word pictures which describe a thing vividly by comparing it with something else.

There are three main types of image:

- **similes** use 'like' or 'as': '... as chaste as is the bud ere it be blown' (*Much Ado About Nothing*)
- **metaphors** are more direct: ''Tut, tut, thou art all ice; thy kindness freezes' (*Richard III*)
- **personifications** describe abstract things as if they were people or gods: 'Let grief and sorrow still embrace his heart/ That doth not wish you joy!' (*The Tempest*)

6 **Sound effects** reinforce meanings by the sounds of words:

- **alliteration**, one sound effect, is the repetition of consonant sounds, as in 'Not a **f**rown **f**urther' (Prospero), linking and emphasising the words.

HELP!

Read verse lines for sense: the sentence may not end at the end of the line.

Remember

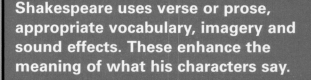

Shakespeare uses verse or prose, appropriate vocabulary, imagery and sound effects. These enhance the meaning of what his characters say.

Copy and complete

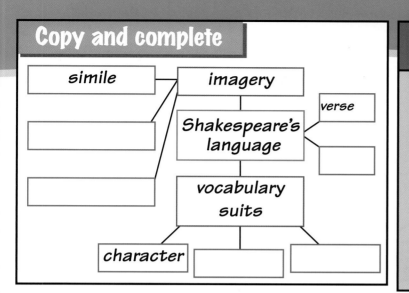

simile — imagery — Shakespeare's language — verse

vocabulary suits

character

2 mins

1 How many syllables are there in a normal line of blank verse?
2 What do Shakespeare's commoners speak in?
3 What kinds of image are these?
   a *Give not this rotten orange to your friend* (*Much Ado about Nothing*)
   b *He receives comfort like cold porridge* (*The Tempest*)
   c *Grim-visaged War hath smooth'd his wrinkled front* (*Richard III*)
4 *'petty pace ...'* What sound effect is used here?

Question and model answer

In the following speech Ariel reports to Prospero on the storm he has raised. Comment on the language.

To every article.   1
I boarded the king's ship; now on the beak,
Now in the waist, the deck, in every cabin,
I flamed amazement: sometime I'd divide,
And burn in many places; on the topmast,   5
The yards and bowsprit, would I flame distinctly,
Then meet and join. Jove's lightnings, the precursors
O' the dreadful thunder-claps, more momentary
And sight-outrunning were not; the fire and cracks
Of sulphurous roaring the most mighty Neptune   10
Seem to besiege and make his bold waves tremble,
Yea, his dread trident shake.

 (*Act 1, Scene 2*)

Now try this!

How does Ariel's language change when Prospero later tells him that there is more to do?

Is there more toil? Since thou dost give me pains,
Let me remember thee what thou hast promised,
Which is not yet perform'd me.

1 Ariel begins by stating simply that he has done exactly what Prospero ordered. The word 'article', referring to an item in a legal contract, shows that he regards himself as bound to Prospero.

2 Although Ariel has been following orders, the energy and delight in his language show that he has enjoyed his work.

3 His repetition of 'now' ('now on the beak,/ Now in the waist) and the list of places where he appeared gives an impression of him being almost in several places at once. The other list – 'the topmast/ The yards and bowsprit' adds to this effect. Both lists end in fire: 'I flamed amazement' and 'would I flame distinctly'. The first, especially, fits Ariel's character since it is a swift way of saying that his flames caused amazement.

4 Line 7 onwards focuses on the power of the storm. Two of the Olympian gods are mentioned. Ariel boasts that his lightning bolts were swifter than those of Jove (Jupiter). His phrase 'sight-outrunning' (faster than the eye can follow) emphasises this. He also claims that his fiery lightning made even the sea god Neptune's waves tremble and his trident (three-pronged weapon) shake.

5 The speech appeals to the senses. We see the lightning, hear the thunder, smell the sulphur (used in gunpowder) and feel the trembling.

Comment

This is a level 7 or 8 answer because it recognises how the speech reflects Ariel's character and mood, comments on the effectiveness of individual words and phrases, and shows an understanding of the language.

Directing scenes

1 **If asked how you would direct two extracts from the play you're studying:**

- Follow the exact **instructions**.
- Show your views on how the extracts could be **interpreted**.
- Imagine them **performed** onstage.
- Be aware that **structure** can influence dramatic effect.
- It may be helpful to **compare** the extracts.

2 **Instructions** could take one of several forms:

- asking about one or more **characters**
- asking about certain aspects of performance, such as a character's **mood**, or the **atmosphere** of the whole extract.

3 *Interpretation:*

- Show your **views**. For example, Caliban might be evil or just misunderstood. A director tells actors to **speak**, **move** and **position** themselves in ways that bring out an interpretation.
- Explain your **reasoning**. For example: 'Caliban's language shows his sensitivity ...'

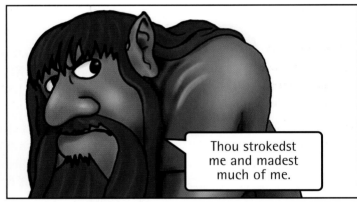

Sound bitter or sad?

Point accusingly?

Thou strokedst me and madest much of me.

Mime stroking?

Speak sarcastically?

4 *Structure:*

- A scene or speech may **develop**, for example building up to a climax.
- A scene may begin with **several** characters and end with just **one** in the spotlight.

5 *The two extracts:*

- It may be helpful to **compare** the extracts, for example if a character's mood changes.
- Be **consistent**. You can show change of mood or a development in the second extract, but not a complete change of character.

The interpretation is up to you, but it must be based on the text. You can direct how actors speak, move and position themselves. Give your reasons.

Work-out!

Copy and complete

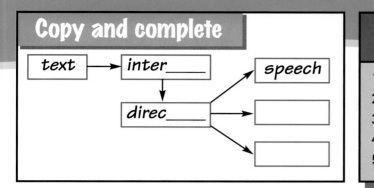

2 mins

1 On what should you base your interpretation?
2 In what three ways does a director direct the actors?
3 What word describes how a scene is built up?
4 What word describes a peak of excitement in a scene?
5 What should you show as well as your directions?

Question and model answer

Read the extract below. Suggest how the actor playing Caliban could show his feelings, giving reasons for your suggestions.

Caliban: This island's mine, by Sycorax my mother,   1
         Which thou takest from me. When thou camest first,
         Thou strokedst me and madest much of me, wouldst give me
         Water with berries in't, and teach me how
         To name the bigger light, and how the less,   5
         That burn by day and night: and then I loved thee
         And show'd thee all the qualities o' the isle,
         The fresh springs, brine-pits, barren place and fertile:
         Cursed be I that did so! All the charms
         Of Sycorax, toads, beetles, bats, light on you!   10
         For I am all the subjects that you have,
         Which first was mine own king: and here you sty me
         In this hard rock, whiles you do keep from me
         The rest o' the island.

(The Tempest, Act 1, Scene 2)

1 Caliban asserts that the island is his by right. The simplicity of his words gives them strength, and the actor should express Caliban's sense of injustice. He could beat his chest on 'mine' for emphasis.

2 From 'When thou ...' (line 2) to 'fertile' (line 8), Caliban is mournful, remembering how Prospero once treated him. To bring this memory alive for the audience, Caliban could point towards the sun ('the bigger light') and the moon ('the less'). He should seem tender at first, then enthusiastic when he lists the 'qualities' of the island, echoing his innocent pleasure in showing them to Prospero.

3 There should be a pause after 'fertile' to allow for Caliban's mood change. He could mark the change by shaking his head in regret, and by folding his arms defensively, because he now hates and fears Prospero.

4 The phrase 'Cursed by I ...' breaks the blank verse rhythm, creating a shock effect, and the next line ('... toads, beetles, bats') is like a magic spell. Caliban is calling on the power of his witch mother.

5 Caliban is both taunting and self-pitying when he says he is Prospero's only subject. The same mixture of bitterness and self-pity is contained in the metaphor 'sty me' (like a pig).

Now try this!

Comment on how the actor playing Prospero should perform his answer to Caliban's lines given above:

Thou most lying slave,
Whom stripes may move, not kindness! I have used thee,
Filth as thou art, with human care, and lodged thee
In mine own cell, till thou didst seek to violate
The honour of my child.

violate: rape

Comments
1 Shows an understanding of Caliban's attitude and how his language shows this.
2 Shows sensitivity to Caliban's character and language and an ability to interpret his words.
3 Recognises the abrupt change of mood, as shown in the language, and suggests an appropriate physical expression of this.
4 Shows a subtle understanding of how Shakespeare uses blank verse.
5 Shows an ability to identify and interpret imagery.

This is a level 7 answer because it selects information, refers to the text, appreciates structure and verse, and offers interpretation.

Answers

Reading

Fiction and non-fiction (page 6)

2 mins

1 Novels and stories
2 Fact
3a Travel writing
3b Autobiography
4 Literary writing
5 Word pictures that make us imagine what is being described.

Now try this!

The direct appeal to the reader's imagination; words that appeal to the senses and imagination: dark, alone, little, trembling, chill, mysterious snufflings, moist gnawings; the metaphor of the 'singing brush' of the bear's side on the tent.

Fact, opinion and bias (page 8)

2 mins

2, 3, 5, 8

Now try this!

A This percentage is only just 'most' (over 50%).
B A negative way of saying that more than half are solved.
C and D are both true only because there are more crimes than ever.
E This sounds good, but the basic crime rate is still increasing.
Types of bias: selection, interpretation.

Meaning and themes (page 10)

2 mins

1a The man burst into tears.
1b Cats avoid water if possible.
2a Men are like children.
2b Irony: the holiday was not a good idea.
3 Friendship, betrayal.

Now try this!

The narrator seems both disgusted by the baby ('that horrible way ... human at all') and sympathetic towards it: he seems relieved when it stops twitching ('at last') and he describes its cries sympathetically ('soft, choked little'). He condemns the man for not doing anything for it, and respects Sham's knowledge of babies.

Values and emotions (page 12)

2 mins

1 Emotive (and rhetorical).
2 That death is preferable to surrender.
3 Neutral language.
4 Word choice.
5 Through characters' action and dialogue.
6 That they are a low form of life and take without giving.

Now try this!

The Native American feels protective towards his people's women and children, and angry towards the 'Wasichu' soldiers. He feels he is completely justified in killing them because they came to his land and attacked his people. This is similar to the girl in the extract in that she is also angry and feels that she would be justified in killing someone who would readily kill her. Both she and the Native American see this as a matter of survival.

Setting and atmosphere (page 14)

2 mins

A Bright dappled, dripping with nectar, exotic plumage, heavy heat, lush foliage, squawking.
B Chill, creaked, dusty, faded, glared malevolently, shadowy.

Characterisation (page 16)

2 mins

1 Direct description.
2 Telling the story through the eyes of one character.
3 That the narrator is jealous of Brian.
4 Dialogue
5 Through action.

Action and mood (page 18)

2 mins

1a Adventure
1b Horror
2 jabbing, flung; slithered, gaping.
3a She burst into the room.
3b A drunk staggered down the road.

Now try this!

There are now two people in the room, and both are awake, not in a nightmare. The mood becomes active and dramatic ('electric shock', 'leaped', 'agitation') rather than having the helpless horror of nightmare.

Narrative viewpoint (page 20)

2 mins

1 A story.
2 First person.
3 Third person.
4 By being the narrator.
5 A narrator cannot give a first-hand account of events he/she does not witness. The language must be realistically 'in character'.

Now try this!

We are led to believe that the narrator is a pupil, and made to share his or her feelings of depression and injustice. The twist is that it turns out to be a teacher.

Persuasive language (page 22)

2 mins

1 Rhetorical question.
2 Repetition
3 Repetition, 'rule of threes', climax.
4 Emotive language.
5 Ironic understatement.
6 Contrast

Now try this!

The use of 'We' includes the reader. The choices are clearly contrasted. The sentence saying what governments did at Kyoto is an example of anticlimax for the purpose of ridicule. The final sentence uses repetition and appeals directly to the reader as 'you'.

Tone (page 24)

2 mins

1 Apologetic
2 Friendly
3 Humorous
4 Sympathetic
5 Angry

Now try this!

Whereas the first author's tone is dignified and stately, and gives no very personal details (only feelings which might be held by many men in his position), the second is much more informal, familiar and self-critical. The author seems to ridicule his own appearance and the illogical nature of his feelings about Limerick.

Figurative language (page 26)

2 mins

1 Simile
2 Personification

3 Analogy
4 Metaphor
5 Simile
6 Personification
7 Metaphor

Structure (page 28)

2 mins

1 The reader's interest.
2 To divide the text up into manageable sections by main ideas.
3 Signpost (signal) a writer's development of ideas.
4 However
5 Therefore; consequently; as a result.

Now try this!

'Similarly' signals a different but closely related point. 'Despite this' signals a point which holds true despite the previous one. 'As a result' signals the consequence of this. 'On the other hand' prepares us for a view which is not quite opposing, but which offers a partial contradiction of the argument so far. In fact, it just adds balance and a note of caution. 'In general, however' prepares us for a conclusion which goes back to the main point: people need more exercise.

Nouns and pronouns (page 30)

2 mins

1a Proper
1b Abstract
1c Concrete
1d Collective
2 A capital letter.
3 Abstract
4 Stand in place of nouns.
5 I

Adjectives (page 32)

2 mins

1 Information about nouns.
2 Quality and quantity.
3 Comparatives
4 Superlatives
5 Nouns
6 Verbs, nouns.

Reading the SATs passages (page 34)

2 mins

Tone: The style used by the writer to establish a particular relationship with the reader.
Mood: The general feeling created by what characters do and say.
Setting: Where part of a story takes place.
Atmosphere:
          The feeling generated by the setting and how it is described.
Narrative viewpoint:
          The point of view from which the story is told.
Imagery: The kind of word pictures used to make the description vivid.
Purpose: The effect that a writer hopes to achieve.
Audience: The intended readership.

Now try this!

1 Rhetorical devices – used in arguing a case.
2 Mood
3 Narrative viewpoint.
4 Purpose and audience. Here, the audience is novice skateboarders. The purpose is to warn or advise.
5 Setting and atmosphere.
6 Imagery
7 Rhetorical devices – this is persuasive writing. (You might also comment on the warning tone, and on the image of 'urban sprawl'.)

Writing

Purpose and audience (page 36)

2 mins

1a To persuade (sell).
1b Persuade
1c Entertain
2 The audience for *Biker's Weekly* would be more specialised than that for the *Daily Mail*. It would probably also have a higher proportion of male readers.
3 Style refers to how language is used for effect; content means the subject matter and the information conveyed.

Word choice: vocabulary and meaning (page 38)

2 mins

1 The range of words whose meaning you know.
2 The apparent, obvious, surface meaning – not any implied or metaphorical one.
3 A meaning hinted at, suggested, not made explicit (obvious).
4 Their connotations and how they work in context.
5 *Menace* hints at something slightly evil, not just risky.
6 *Happy* sounds more upbeat and lively, and perhaps more short-lived. *Contented* is calmer, like someone sitting in an armchair rather than jumping about.

Now try this!

That was his most **brilliant** idea of heaven's happiness: mine was rocking in a rustling green tree, with a west wind blowing, and bright, white clouds flitting **rapidly** above; and not only larks, but throstles, and blackbirds, and linnets, and cuckoos **pouring** out music on every side, and the moors seen at a distance, broken into cool dusky dells; but close by great swells of long grass **undulating** in waves to the breeze; and woods and sounding water, and the whole world awake and wild with joy.

Qualifiers (page 40)

2 mins

1 Ordinary, innocently, normally.
2 In ascending order: hardly, slightly, partly,

fairly, extremely, totally, mind-bogglingly, infinitely. ('totally' and 'mind-bogglingly' could be reversed, although in theory nothing can be more than total – except infinite!)

3 Understatement and exaggeration.

Now try this!

totally (or absolutely), nearly, incredibly, pathetically, pretty, astonishingly, absolutely (or totally)

Making sense: clauses and punctuation (page 42)

2 mins

1a Duncan (subject) rides (verb) a bike (object).

1b Horses (subject) love (verb) sugar lumps (object).

1c I (subject) don't eat (verb) meat (object).

2 An exclamation.

3 My PC, being two years old, has no CD writer.

4 I'm tired, so I'm going to sleep.

Now try this!

She wore an overcoat which had once been pink but which was now uniformly grey. On her head was a beret which had been donated by a schoolgirl who had taken pity on her. Her possessions, which didn't amount to much, were bundled into a supermarket trolley and were soaking wet.

Colons, semicolons and dashes (page 44)

2 mins

1a Here's my theory: the butler did it.

1b Three reasons: it's cold, it's wet and I'm tired.

2a To make mistakes is human; to forgive them is divine.

2b Facilities include: squash courts; a pool, sauna and jacuzzi; and a fitness suite.

3a The intruder – if there had ever been one – was gone.

3b Get out of here – scram!

Now try this!

An 11-year-old boy had a narrow escape: in a field – not far from his home – he spotted what he thought was his pet cat in long grass. Going to stroke it, he soon found his head in the jaws of a black panther. An expert later explained: it was playing with the boy. Another expert advised anyone encountering a big cat:

don't scream or run – this could provoke an attack; keep still; remain standing to assert dominance; let the animal wander off.

Passive sentences, tenses, ambiguity (page 46)

2 mins

1a Eric was eaten by a lion.

1b My lunch box was run over by a bus.

2a Everyone ignores her.

2b A bee stung me.

3 Present

4 'his' – is it the father's or the uncle's?

Now try this!

William landed near modern-day Hastings. The Norman knights on horseback charged the Saxons, but the Saxons fought bravely and almost won. Things went downhill for them after Harold was hit in the eye by an arrow. If it hadn't been for this, English history might have turned out very differently.

Formal and informal English (page 48)

2 mins

1 So they can be understood by as many English speakers as possible.

2 Regional and social groups.

3 If you had asked me I would have, but now I will not.

4 Vocabulary, grammar, idioms.

5 In dialogue.

Now try this!

I was just relaxing when I heard a commotion outside. I ran out onto the street and saw a man hitting a boy. I said to him, 'Stop hitting the boy!' He replied, 'Are you joking?' Then a police officer came and the man ran off.

Paragraphing (page 50)

2 mins

1 Introduce your piece and catch the reader's interest.

2 Draw your ideas to a conclusion.

3 Often

4 Chronologically; in order of importance.

Structuring a story (page 52)

2 mins

1 Action, character detail, dialogue.

2 The development.

3 The story would be dull without one.

4 What's going to happen next.

5 A sense of completion/closure.

Telling the story: narrative devices (page 54)

2 mins

1 Reveal or withhold it.

2 First person.

3 Present

4 Commentary; what they do; what they say.

5 Flashback

Commentary, description and dialogue (page 56)

2 mins

1 Dialogue

2 It can slow the pace too much.

3 A purpose (and speech marks!).

4a 'We're lost,' she said. He told her not to worry.

4b 'How can we survive?' I asked.

Inform, explain, describe (page 58)

2 mins

1 Putting yourself in his or her shoes.

2 Details and examples.

3 Repeated and irrelevant information.

4 The least important bits.

5 When giving examples.

Persuade, argue, advise (page 60)

2 mins

1 To explore your own ideas and be prepared for counter-arguments.

2 Statistics (but there are others).

3 Certainly

4 Nice

5 When giving advice.

Analyse, review, comment (page 62)

2 mins

1 To decide whether or not to read the book.

2 The evidence.

3 They are open-ended (and therefore could be used in giving advice).

4 Personally

5 When giving an alternative viewpoint.

Spelling: vowel rules (page 64)

2 mins

1　Dining
2　Winning
3　Shinning
4　It makes it long.
5　Double the consonant before the new endings; e.g. matting, not mating.
6　Seize, weird.

Now try this!

Darren was **taking** his time over his **homework**. He was **determined** not to make any **mistakes**. He'd **received** a low mark and was **hoping** to do better. **Unfortunately** he'd **slopped** coffee all over it. He **hated** maths. His teacher said he could be a **shining** example to the class if he tried, instead of **sitting** in the corner **moping** over his **misfortunes**.

Plurals, verbs and apostrophes (page 66)

2 mins

1a　The two babies' cries came to the women's ears.
1b　We've had dingoes in our studios!
1c　Buses travel in convoys.
2　By adding 'es'.
3　To show possession or omission.
4　three o'clock
5　Dialogue

Prefixes, suffixes and homophones (page 68)

2 mins

1　Preview
2　Forearm
3　Inactive, unfair, irregular, imprecise.
4　Inspiration, perspiration, promotion.
5　Drinkable, terrible.
6　Have a quiet night.

Now try this!

comfortable, passable, believable, fashionable, laughable, drinkable, inedible, incredible, horrible, terrible, forcible, indelible, divisible, insoluble, accommodation, necessary, traveller, beautiful.

Shakespeare

Shakespeare's world (page 70)

2 mins

Any points relating to: class divisions (less pronounced now); status of women (better now); travel (easier now); health (better now – no plague); beliefs (more uncertain now); entertainment (mass media technology).

Now try this!

The Tempest: people believed in the power of magic and that the dead were in a sense sleeping (waiting for Judgement Day)

Richard III: Armies engaged in hand-to-hand fighting with simple weapons. People were more patriotic and obeyed their king.

Much Ado About Nothing: Women were seen as the property of men, and were expected to be pure and innocent before marriage.

History, comedy, tragedy (page 72)

2 mins

1　*Macbeth* very loosely; *Twelfth Night* no; *Henry V* yes.
2　*Twelfth Night* no; others yes.
3　*Henry V* yes; others no.
4　Only in *Macbeth*.
5　Yes for *Twelfth Night* and *Henry V*.
6　*Macbeth* the Witches' prediction; *Twelfth Night* Viola and Sebastian being shipwrecked (you could add Malvolio's slighting of Sir Toby and friends for the subplot); *Henry V* Henry deciding that he can legally claim the throne of France.
7　*Macbeth* murders, war; *Twelfth Night* trickery, confusions, disguises; *Henry V* war.
8　*Macbeth* Macbeth killed by Macduff and replaced as king by Malcolm; *Twelfth Night* confusions cleared up, three marriages; *Henry V* Henry beating France and marrying Katharine as part of the peace settlement.

Plot and themes in a tragedy (page 74)

2 mins

1　The Witches.
2　Flee (Malcolm to England).
3　So that he can grow up and have a son who will become the first of many kings

descended from Banquo – thus fulfilling the prophecy.
4　Macduff
5　Herself
6　Evil; Courage; Deception; Order; Disorder.

Plot and themes in a comedy (page 76)

2 mins

1　Benedick
2　Don John
3　Don Pedro (for Claudio)
4　Hero
5　Beatrice
6　Margaret
7　The constables overhear him boasting.
8　Don Pedro

Plot and themes in a history (page 78)

2 mins

1　The French throne.
2　The English throne.
3　Three traitors (Scroop, Grey and Cambridge).
4　His brother Clarence.
5　Henry wins the war with France and is to marry Katharine.
6　Richmond kills Richard in battle and is to become the new king.

Characterisation in a tragedy (page 80)

2 mins

1　Duncan
2　Banquo
3　Lady Macbeth
4　Macduff's
5　Malcolm
6　Macbeth wants to avoid evil. He respects the bonds of family, hospitality and loyalty to his king (he is Duncan's 'kinsman', 'host' and 'subject'). He feels it would be a great sin to kill so 'meek' and virtuous a man.

Now try this!

In the first speech he is being decisive, dynamic and ruthless. In the second all this dynamism has disappeared. He is depressed

Answers

and sees life as completely pointless and meaningless. Note the slow repetition of 'Tomorrow', the image of life as a 'tale told by an idiot', etc. (See also 'Shakespeare's language', page 88.)

Characterisation in a comedy (page 82)

2 mins

1 Don John
2 Benedick
3 Hero
4 Beatrice
5 Claudio
6 Benedick
7 Leonato

Now try this!

On both occasions Claudio has been easily fooled by Don John into misjudging someone. That he trusts Don John, a known villain with a grudge against him, shows he is naive. His first mistake prepares us for his being fooled more seriously next time. In the first speech, he is disappointed but seems to accept his loss. He blames himself for letting Don Pedro 'negotiate' on his behalf, but he also says that 'beauty is a witch'. In the second speech, his disappointment is more bitter. In the first speech, he sees women as temptresses luring men away from loyal friendship; in the second, he sees them as even worse – cunning, sinful deceivers.

Characterisation in a history (page 84)

2 mins

1 A civil war.
2 Anne.
3 He is deformed.
4 Villianously.
5 He has the young Princes murdered.
6 He orders his execution.
7 'God's enemy'.
8 Richard's brother.

Now try this!

In Act 5, Scene 3 Richard is tormented by doubts and fears, but when he woos Anne he is cynically calm and collected. This enables him to be ruthlessly manipulative, even arguing persuasively that he murdered Anne's husband

out of love for her. After she goes, he revels in his own powers of manipulation.

Shakespeare: writing in role (page 86)

2 mins

1 Two extracts.
2 Tone
3a *Macbeth*: Macbeth in Act 5, when the doctor has reported his wife's madness.
3b Benedick at the end of Act 2, scene 3, when he starts to fall in love with Beatrice.
3c *The Tempest*: Prospero in Act 5, Scene 1, when he has to release Ariel, as promised.
3d Buckingham, in Act 5, scene 1, when he is about to be executed.

Shakespeare's language (page 88)

2 mins

1 Ten (five pairs)
2 Prose
3a Metaphor
3b Simile
3c Personification
4 Alliteration

Now try this!

Ariel's language loses its enthusiasm, energy and colourful imagery and begins to sound resentful, especially with the words 'toil' and 'pains'.

Directing scenes (page 90)

2 mins

1 The evidence of the play.
2 On how they speak, move and position themselves.
3 Its 'structure'.
4 Climax
5 Your reasons.

Now try this!

Prospero is bitter because he once trusted Caliban and felt affection for him. He feels betrayed by Caliban and cannot forgive his attempt to rape Miranda. Hence he should show disgust and anger when he calls Caliban 'lying slave', perhaps threatening him on the line 'Whom stripes may move' (meaning whipping may persuade). Prospero could express a sense of righteous indignation, as if he was once more kind to Caliban than was justified, given that he is not exactly human. He could spread his arms wide on 'In mine own cell' to give a sense of how he sees his own generosity to Caliban. He should almost spit out the word 'violate', as he sees Caliban's crime as unforgivable, and by contrast could lay his hand protectively on Miranda on the final line.